T0375719

True North

A FLICKERING SOUL IN NO MAN'S LAND

ABOUT THE CAREER OF
Knut Utstein Kloster FATHER OF THE $40-BILLION-A-YEAR MODERN CRUISE INDUSTRY

Second Edition Revised and Updated

STEPHANIE GALLAGHER   FOREWORD BY JAMES LOVELOCK

iUniverse, Inc.
Bloomington

True North
A Flickering soul in no man's land; Knut Utstein Kloster, father of the $40-billion-a-year modern cruise industry

Second Edition – Revised and Updated

iUniverse books may be ordered through booksellers or by contacting:

iUniverse
1663 Liberty Drive
Bloomington, IN 47403
www.iuniverse.com
1-800-Authors (1-800-288-4677)

Because of the dynamic nature of the Internet, any web addresses or links contained in this book may have changed since publication and may no longer be valid. The views expressed in this work are solely those of the author and do not necessarily reflect the views of the publisher, and the publisher hereby disclaims any responsibility for them.

ISBN: 978-1-4620-4150-3 (sc)
ISBN: 978-1-4620-4151-0 (hc)
ISBN: 978-1-4620-4152-7 (e)

Printed in the United States of America

iUniverse rev. date: 08/04/2011

For

My loving husband Charles

In fondest memory of our dear friend and colleague,

John S. Rogers

With deepest gratitude to and affection

for the late Admiral J. William Kime (U.S.C.G.)

"Onwards, Upwards, Excelsior" to the creative brilliance of

Naval Architect Tage Wandborg

and

Special thanks to Marine Engineer Richard (Dick) Baumler

CONTENTS

FOREWORD
By James Lovelock

Over the last forty-four years, I have developed a scientific theory known as Gaia — named after the Greek goddess of Earth. It was the Nobel Laureate novelist, William Golding, who suggested the name Gaia. Under the Gaian theory, all life on Earth and all material parts of the Earth's surface — the air, the oceans, the rocks, and all living organisms — evolved together as a single, inseparable self-regulating system, a living planet. This "living Earth" is able to regulate its climate and composition so as always to be comfortable for the organisms that inhabit it. The Gaia Theory forces a planetary perspective in which humankind is merely part of the whole. It is the health of the planet that matters, not some individual species of organisms. The health of the Earth is now threatened by major changes in natural ecosystems, and we know that humankind bears responsibility for some of this damage. Agriculture and forestry, for example, are seen as serious sources of this kind of damage with the inexorable increase in greenhouse gases, carbon dioxide and methane. Many believe that human activity is associated with, even responsible for, global heating.

Stephanie Gallagher's sensitive and beautifully composed book tells the life story of a remarkable and honourable man, Knut Utstein Kloster. His farsighted vision of a better world and a life spent working to make it possible puts us all in his debt. Kloster touched my life by his unstinted support for Gaia. He also sponsored an important environmental mission in 1991-1992 by sending a replica Viking ship named *GAIA* across the oceans and to the Earth Summit in Rio, gathering messages from the world's children along the vessel's 15,000 mile journey (Chapter Six). I was present in Port Canaveral with Astronaut Jim Lovell to bid *GAIA* a safe passage to Rio.

Kloster is more optimistic than I am. In my most recent book (2009), *The Vanishing Face of Gaia: A Final Warning*, I argue that human beings have already triggered an imminent and unavoidable rapid warming of the planet to the point that it will be able to support fewer of us. So, even though he didn't plan it that way, Kloster's concept of "world cities" at sea holds special appeal; I see them as future lifeboats for a civilization that, hopefully, will learn to live *with* — as opposed to *against* — Mother Nature. I see them as self-sustaining communities that farm the ocean for their needs and in a way that does not threaten the Earth, unlike our land-based civilization.

Kloster's floating cities (Chapters Four and Five) are meant to combine pleasure and purpose, capitalism with a conscience, profit-making with social and environmental responsibility, and based on what I know of this man, he will succeed and I applaud the initiative, in particular the ultimate goal of creating clean, green, environmentally benign global villages (Chapter Nine).

With nearly three quarters of the Earth covered by ocean and with rising sea levels, climate refugees are already flooding into *real* lifeboats — islands and peninsulas which may soon be overcrowded beyond endurance. So whether you believe, as Kloster does, that there is still hope for life as we know it here on Earth, or believe as I do that more and more lifeboats will be needed, it's a perfect time to realize Kloster's vision of ships that are cities at sea — worlds unto themselves, self-sustaining human-scale communities that accept Gaia's rules, rather than waging war against them.

James Lovelock is an independent scientist, inventor, and author of several books, including *The Vanishing Face of Gaia: A Final Warning* (2009), *The Revenge of Gaia* (2006), *Homage to Gaia* (2000), *Gaia: The Practical Science of Planetary Medicine* (1991), *The Ages of Gaia* (1988), and *Gaia, A New Look at Life on Earth* (1979). He has been an Honorary Visiting Fellow of Green Templeton College, University of Oxford since 1994 and the recipient of many honors and awards, and was made a Companion of Honour in 2002 by Her Majesty the Queen (United Kingdom).

ACKNOWLEDGEMENTS

First I would like to acknowledge the kind cooperation of my subject, Knut Utstein Kloster. As I note in the Preface, it has been difficult for him to be in the limelight, to have the cameras focused on him, to be praised. But I do praise him. I praise his work, his career, his kindness, his caring, his commitment, and, mostly, his example.

Many of the activities described in this book were the product of a team effort. I acknowledge with great affection and admiration the hard work and dedication of Knut's principal partners, Tage Wandborg, John S. Rogers, Admiral J. William Kime, Richard Baumler and many others.

I thank my husband, Charles, for his patience and proofreading, as well as his many constructive suggestions as to the content and tone of the book. Also Tage Wandborg and Richard Baumler. Special thanks to Liv Myhre for her Norwegian-to-English translation of some of the articles and speeches used in the book, for her valued editorial comments, and insight into Norway's Jante Law (see Preface).

Chapters Four and Five relate to the revolutionary Phoenix concept and the American Flagship project — a story unto itself. That will be my next book. But I have used this Second Edition to update readers on that important national project and would like to again thank the hundreds of people who have supported the Build America initiative with their creativity, time and talent, particularly Hon. Helen Delich Bentley, Charles D. Brown, H. Clayton Cook, Joe La Polla, C. James Patti, Bruce Roberts and Charles (Chuck) Rowland, to name just a few.

Barbara Colasuonno, Creative Director of Group 33 Design Associates, Inc., has once again proven her graphic design skills and considerable talents as an editor and proofreader in helping to bring this Second Edition of True North to fruition.

PREFACE

In Norway, they have something called the Jante Law: "Du skal ikke tro at du *er* noe." Freely translated, it means "Don't think that you *are* anything."

The "law" derives from a novel by a Norwegian/Danish author, Aksel Sandemose. The book takes place in an imaginary Danish small town called Jante and describes what the author sees as the unspoken rules of such communities in general. Jante law conveys an important element of Norwegian culture: humility. It teaches people to be modest and to try and see all people as being on equal footing. Norwegians, at least historically, do not flaunt their wealth or financial achievements and look askance at those who do.

Essentially, the main tenets of Jante Law are:

- You shall not think you are special.
- You shall not believe you are smarter than others.
- You shall not believe you are wiser than others.
- You shall not behave as if you are better than others.
- You shall not believe that you know more than others.

- You shall not believe that you can fix things better than others.
- You shall not believe that you can teach others anything.

Norwegians have an egalitarian outlook; they generally express themselves in very modest terms when it comes to compliments and praises. They like people for themselves and not for what they do for a living or for how much money they earn. While this collectivist tradition is gradually giving way to more individualistic values, the concept of Jante Law is still strong in Norway today. Any form of elitism is likely to be met with criticism.

Having explained that characteristic of Norwegian society and culture, the author acknowledges that her Norwegian subject, Knut Utstein Kloster, has been very uncomfortable with this process. He is embarrassed by the attention on himself; he does not think he is special; he does not think he is smarter, wiser, or better than others; he doesn't think he knows more than others or that he can fix things better than others — but I do — and that is why I have chosen to write this story. I think Knut's life, career, concerns and motivations offer an inspiration, a focus on the possible, and an example to be followed.

Knut answered my questions, shared some stories, and provided some of the photographs in this book; but he's not happy to be its subject. He's Norwegian, head to toe, in and out. He thinks he can't teach anybody anything. I think my readers will disagree.

In writing this Second Edition, I asked Knut if there was anything in particular that he would like to add to the story or change if he could. I asked him whether the American Flagship project — after such a long gestation period — still resonated for him now that so many of the ideas and innovations introduced in the context of the project have been emulated by the cruise industry. Acknowledging that the city-ship project was ahead of its time, he deferred to Shakespeare: "There is a tide in the affairs of men which, taken at the flood, leads on to fortune...and we must take the current when it serves or lose our ventures."

Not that Knut thinks the venture will be lost, but he suggests that if the United States cannot muster the political will to now propel this private-sector developed project into realization — in light of its obvious benefits to that nation in terms of job creation, tax revenue generation, and trade deficit reduction — it doesn't mean that the Phoenix project can't rise in a different part of the world, or be built elsewhere and reflagged by means of a Passenger Vessel Services Act (PVSA) exemption, as was done for the NCL America ships in Hawaii.

Indeed, for many years, the World City team has viewed Asia, particularly China, as an ideal market for the city-ship concept and have a well-developed plan for introducing *DRAGON WORLD CITY* to China's rising middle class within the next five years. I was perhaps remiss in not including the *DRAGON WORLD CITY* initiative — in which a great deal of work, time, and money has been invested — in the First Edition. That omission has been corrected in this Second Edition (Chapter Eleven).

I have also used this revision to talk a little more about Knut's interesting idea for a Little United Nations At Sea (LUNAS) (Chapter Ten). Knut has been thinking about LUNAS since the 1980s when he asked the (then) Secretary General of the United Nations, Hon. Kurt Waldheim, for permission to fly the

UN flag onboard the *S/S NORWAY*. With its diverse nationalities of officers, passengers and crew, Knut saw the *S/S NORWAY* as a little United Nations and he began thinking about a ship dedicated to the goals of that organization, on a global track, promoting world peace and understanding, and bridging the gap between developed and emerging nations.

Knut is just as uncomfortable with this Second Edition of the book as he was with the First Edition. Also, he questioned whether it wouldn't be better to wait until the American Flagship is contracted to update his story. While this Second Edition may be premature as it relates to Chapter Five, I believe that my readers — many of whom are decision-makers in Washington — would prefer to read about the current status of that project and also benefit from the additional information I have provided on the Title XI program and the few remaining steps needed to finally move the American Flagship project forward to contract.

INTRODUCTION

*Above all, unto thine own self be true and it shall follow as
the day the night, thou can'st not then be false to any man.*
Shakespeare — *Hamlet*

Our story is about a visionary man with an impressive career
spanning five decades: Knut Utstein Kloster.

Knut is a Norwegian, generally considered the father or
founder of the modern cruise industry — an industry which
today generates over $40 billion in annual revenues. He is a man
of conscience, with a world view. He once described himself as a
"flickering soul" in no man's land — the place where his world is
secure and comfortable, but where, just beyond reach and in full
sight, over 4 billion people live in abject poverty, suffering from
preventable diseases, and subsisting without basic necessities,
most without even electricity.

Globalization and the information age have combined to

make the world a very small place where it is more difficult to blur the misery of others or to any longer pretend there is nothing we can do about it. Industrialization of the rich and developed countries has unwittingly contributed enormously to the degradation of the planet, and now our bad example is being replicated by aspiring developing nations and their exploding populations. Knut has never been able to put these realities out of his mind or to conduct his life or operate his business ventures as if they are disconnected from what is happening to the planet and billions of its less fortunate inhabitants. More of us need to feel that connection if civilization, as we know it, is to be sustained.

Knut was Chairman of Klosters Rederi A/S which operated a fleet of cargo ships; he developed an innovative plan for port decongestion that unblocked one of the busiest ports in the world in the 70s and provided a prototype for other developing nations; he founded Norwegian Caribbean Lines (NCL), later renamed Norwegian Cruise Line. Klosters Rederi A/S also owned, for a period, Royal Viking Line and Royal Cruise Line.

Knut played an important role in the 1994 Winter Olympics at Lillehammer, Norway, by developing a traditional Norwegian village, with sod-roofed cottages in designs dating back over the centuries, to house the international media covering the event. The village also contained a large community center which served as the media's headquarters during the games. The government of Norway had insisted that every aspect of the planning for the Olympics conform to the highest possible environmental standards and that all development projects would have a useful life after the games. Today, that mountain village is enjoyed year round by Norwegian families and tourists and is a great asset for the region.

Kloster sponsored a 15,000 mile journey of a replica Viking ship, named *GAIA* after Mother Earth, which gathered thousands of messages of children along her route and delivered them to world leaders in Rio for the 1992 Earth Summit/Global Forum. For decades, Knut has promoted a concept for a Little United Nations at Sea (LUNAS). A new Chapter Ten has been added to talk more about this interesting initiative.

This is not a biography but rather career highlights. Much of the story takes place around Kloster's $1.5 billion "city-ship" project, initially known as the "Phoenix project." The Phoenix project spotlights Knut's vision, pioneering spirit, willingness to take risks, and perseverance in the face of seemingly insurmountable obstacles. It also epitomizes the ideal that businesses can have a heart and make a difference and that financial and larger goals can complement one another.

What is particularly exciting about the Phoenix project is its scale and innovation. Although the ship is not yet contracted, the correctness of Knut's vision has already been proven out in the cruise industry. He was *right* when everyone said he was *wrong*, it was *possible* when everyone said it *wasn't,* and decades after he correctly projected where the industry was heading, and how powerfully it would contribute to the international leisure travel business, the project is poised for realization. When the prototype ship is built, it will be all that Knut envisioned it to be, not only an outstanding financial success, but, most importantly, a model of 21st century capitalism.

Whether we call it, as Bill Gates does, "creative capitalism," or as Whole Foods' founder John Mackey does, "conscious capitalism," the new bottom line for 21st century capitalism will measure success based on the company's impact on *all* stakeholders, including the environment and the global community at large.

With marine pollution playing a significant role in the destruction of our environment and ocean ecosystem, Knut has helped launch a Green Clean Global Village® initiative which will promote green technologies for ships including, where appropriate, advanced nuclear propulsion that might ultimately enable ships to be operated profitably — with zero emissions — in harmony with nature. Kloster's vision for the ships of the future includes insuring that they operate with minimum impact on the environment.

Throughout his interesting career and challenging business ventures, he has proven the axiom that businesses can "do well by doing good."

Long before green became more than a color, or capitalism came generally to mean more than just profit-making, Knut was investing in socially responsible enterprises that valued all of its stakeholders. The now popular expression, "triple bottom line," was Knut's *modus operandi* from day one. He actively supported the earliest initiatives aimed at improving the environment and promoting the concepts of sustainable development, such as the *Centre for our Common Future*, that took up, on a private level, the excellent work of The World Commission on Environment and Development which had been headed up by former Norwegian Prime Minister, Hon. Gro Harlem Brundtland.

This book highlights some of Knut Utstein Kloster's major business ventures in which he strove to combine financial and larger goals: "2 + 2 = 5," he said, and the formula has guided most of his business decisions from an early age. The story emphasizes the important role of the conscience in navigating a just and equitable course forward. Kloster's "no man's land" is the distance between the world-*that-is* and the world-*as-it-should be.*

You don't have to know or care anything at all about shipping or about the cruise business to enjoy and be inspired by this story. Knut happened to descend from an old and respected shipping family in Norway, so it follows (particularly after the early death of his father) that he stayed in the family business and, as a highly intelligent, restless and adventuresome young man, set out to build on his experience and expand the business in new and exciting directions.

To be touched by this man's life and example, it could have been any other business, but it actually helps the story that Knut is in shipping because of its international character. It is a business in which the stakes are often high, the risks can be immense, and the potential for change and innovation is wide open. Since the oceans represent 70% of the Earth's surface and are, like the skies above, imperiled by pollution and other human activity, Knut's leadership in this area is especially important.

The story about the creation and development of the modern day cruise industry has actually been told very well by Kristoffer A. Garin in his 2005 book, *Devils on the Deep Blue Sea.* Knut wasn't, by the way, one of the "devils" in Garin's book; indeed, he was one of the few angels. But Garin's vivid and mostly accurate tale about what has become the fastest growing sector of the leisure travel industry confirms the point that, as an industry, the cruise business provides an exciting backdrop for the story to be told in these pages and for formulating solutions to many of our planet's problems.

Years ago, Knut was given the nickname "True North" because it best described his "true to self/true to values" character and life qualities. No question, this is a man who seems to be guided by a brighter star, pulled by some magnetic force to caring, and driven by an honesty of purpose that all too frequently eludes many of the rest of us in our busy preoccupied daily lives. Thus, his story is inspiring and encouraging. Guided by his internal compass, Knut dares to navigate uncharted waters, to set his sights on the possible. His business ventures are exciting and demonstrate that entrepreneurialism and larger goals can go hand-in-hand and benefit one another.

CHAPTER ONE
Seeing the Future — and Going For It

Some people are born visionaries — they see the future, both its prospects and its potential problems. Seeing the future enables one to take action, to take risks, and to make decisions which capitalize on the prospects and, with some planning and luck, hopefully steer clear of the problems.

Knut Utstein Kloster is such a visionary, not only about the prospects and potential pitfalls of his business ventures, but also in the larger sense, in terms of the human condition and the state of the world.

"Set your course by distant stars, not by the light of passing ships." This is one of his favorite sayings. And that is what he has done his whole life.

Knut was barely 30 years of age when his father died and he therefore took the helm of the family shipping business in Oslo. He had been educated in the United States at the Massachusetts Institute of Technology (MIT) in naval architecture and marine engineering.

In 1964, questioning the need for diversification of his company's cargo fleet, Knut commissioned an advanced, specially-designed passenger-and-car liner. The plan was to engage the ship in weekly service between Southampton and Gibraltar, with calls at Vigo, Spain and Lisbon, Portugal. Tourists could take their cars on the ship or have the option of driving down and cruising back on a seven-day round trip schedule.

This is a good time to introduce Knut's closest collaborator, Tage Wandborg, likely the world's greatest and surely its most prolific naval architect. A Dane, Tage was entrusted to convert Kloster's vision into steel. At that time, Tage was working as Chief Designer in a Copenhagen-based consulting naval architecture firm. He was an innovator and trendsetter in the construction of passenger-and-car liners all over the world.

The first 'cruise' ship

Tage Wandborg was asked by Kloster to design a large, purpose-built passenger-and-car liner that could provide a safe and comfortable ride for passengers en route to the Mediterranean via the often-stormy waters of the Bay of Biscay.

The result was a highly advanced, efficient and futuristic yacht-style liner which was to pioneer the modern cruise industry. The ship was built in Norway and named *M/S SUNWARD*.

The operation of *M/S SUNWARD* started in 1966 and was a great success, *at first*. Then two things happened which changed the economic prospects of the enterprise dramatically. The United Kingdom enacted a law that restricted the currency

NCL's M/S SUNWARD was an ultra modern, highly efficient, yacht-style passenger-and-car liner.

which U.K. citizens could take out of the country, and Spain's General Franco closed the frontier between Spain and Gibraltar, meaning the U.K. tourists couldn't get past the border into Spain.

Meanwhile, in Miami, Ted Arison (who later founded Carnival Cruise Lines) was marketing two Israeli-owned car ferries on short cruises to the Bahamas. The sudden bankruptcy of the Israeli shipowners and arrest of their ships by creditors had left Arison with booked passengers but no ship.

At this point, Arison learned of the fate of Kloster's U.K.-to-Spain passenger-and-car ferry service and of the possible availability of the ultra-modern *M/S SUNWARD*. Arison contacted Kloster who made a quick decision to transfer the ship to Miami and engage her in three and four day cruises to the Bahamas.

Always with foresight, Kloster had ordered a ship with air

Here we see the pioneering M/S SUNWARD in Southampton, summer 1966, in the company of some of Britain's most famous liners.

conditioning capacity, in case she would ultimately serve in warmer climates. Every cabin had private facilities which were quite unusual for passenger-and-car ferries at that time. Ted Arison became the agent of Klosters Rederi A/S. A new company was formed, Norwegian Caribbean Lines (NCL), to operate the ship.

M/S SUNWARD sailed a few weeks later from Miami on a 1966 Christmas cruise. The operation of the ship in the Caribbean trade was an immediate success.

Off and running — M/S STARWARD and M/S SKYWARD

Six months later, Kloster asked Tage Wandborg to design the optimum cruise ship for this new market. However, Knut indicated that he still wanted the new ships to have some roll-on/roll-off freight capacity, in case of a change in the demand for cruises. Orders were placed with a German shipyard in Bremerhaven, and the ships were later christened *M/S STARWARD* and *M/S SKYWARD*.

The new ships were to be 12,940 GRT,* with a capacity for 540 passengers and 220 cars or other vehicles. Halfway into the building period, with the demand for cruises on *M/S SUNWARD* greatly exceeding capacity, Knut asked Tage if he could change the design, mid-construction, to exclude the freight capacity and to add more passenger capacity. Tage arranged a meeting with the shipyard and presented his design suggestions for eliminating the freight capacity and adding more guest cabins. The yard accepted the proposal and the first purpose-built cruise ship (delivered on time and on budget) was successfully introduced into the Caribbean market.

Full speed ahead — M/S SOUTHWARD and M/S SEAWARD

Success breeds success and two sister ships of *M/S STARWARD* and *M/S SKYWARD* were ordered by Kloster from an Italian shipyard. When Tage learned of Knut's order for the newbuilds, he informed Knut that there was an opportunity to introduce still further design innovations which would make the ships even more appealing and appropriate for the cruise market. Knut and Tage traveled to Italy to see if the yard could be persuaded to alter the contract design in accordance with Tage's further design innovations. The yard recognized that it would enhance

---

*GRT means gross registered tons (a measure of cubic space).

their own reputation to introduce such future-oriented cruise ships and the plan was accepted without a change in budget. The two new ships were to be named *M/S SOUTHWARD* and *M/S SEAWARD*.

Then the glitch — but honor above all

Shortly before the two new ships were to be delivered by the state-owned Italian shipyard, Kloster received a disturbing message from the shipyard that both contracts had been cancelled. The contract for each ship had been $13 million and advance bookings had already been made for both ships. The yard referred to some statutory provision from the Mussolini era which permitted a state-owned facility to cancel a contract that resulted in the state losing money. Lawyers were dispatched to Italy. In a private meeting with a government official, NCL's lawyers were told that one million dollars to a numbered Swiss bank account would resolve the matter. There is probably no need to tell my readers, even this early on in the story, that Knut was not about to wire money into a Swiss bank account. "It was morally and legally impossible," he said.

After lengthy negotiations, the *M/S SOUTHWARD* was delivered on budget, but the second ship, *M/S SEAWARD*, was, instead, sold for $20 million to P & O, and became the *SPIRIT OF LONDON* — a costly setback for NCL. For Knut, it was a matter of conscience, "an unsettling affair, but forget it and move on."

With the delivery of *M/S SOUTHWARD*, Kloster had four ships delivered within four years — and the modern cruise industry was born.

Growth continues — SUNWARD II

In 1973, Knut decided to sell the passenger-and-car ferry, *M/S SUNWARD*, and to acquire a vessel with additional passenger capacity to meet ever-increasing demand. It was learned that the *CUNARD ADVENTURE* was for sale. Coincidentally, Tage Wandborg had designed this ship for another client, but when Cunard acquired it, a different naval architect was retained to change the exterior of the ship so that it would replicate the sheer lines of Cunard's *QE II*.

Knut asked Tage to redesign the ship so that it would match the futuristic yacht-style of the other NCL ships, now known as the "white fleet." After the conversion, the ship was christened *M/S SUNWARD II*.

"Kloster — A Modern Shipowner"

In 1971, when Knut was visiting Genoa for the sea trials of the *M/S SOUTHWARD*, reporters from the local newspaper, *Ritratti*, interviewed him. The headline of the article was "Kloster — A Modern Shipowner." Of course, there was no mention in the article about the cancellation of the contract for of the *M/S SEAWARD*. But the *Ritratti* article (roughly translated) captures the essence of the man:

> Talking with the reporters on board, he [Kloster] has made some comments about the working conditions in the Italian factories.
>
> "The workers are not treated well," he said. "I don't mean economically, they can earn good money, but they don't feel respected in the factory…the workers must only obey orders without any possibility of telling their opinions…"

Who is this Norwegian gentleman? He cannot be similarly compared to our own shipowners.

His name is Knut, a navigator's name, he is 42 years old, about 1 meter and 90 centimeters tall, handsome and athletically perfect. He is the third generation of the Kloster family of Oslo, a family that has owned ships since 1905. He is an intelligent man with quick answers…He works seriously at his profession. He is a naval architect, which he studied to be at the Massachusetts Institute of Technology in Boston in the United States. Courteous and precise, he answers all questions without difficulty. But as soon as the opportunity comes, he is quick to ask the questions.

"You want to know me? Good. I want to know you, too. Let's talk about things that interest us both."

We spoke about books. This Norwegian shipowner reads methodically every day, not only those books that are of interest to his profession. Flying from Miami, he spent his time reading *The Revue of the Merchant Marine*, regarding ships, and *The Greening of America*, an historical-sociological book written by a Yale professor. It is not the first time he read this book. "This is a really marvelous book. It gave me an answer to a question that I have been thinking about for a long time. I have asked myself many times — Where is the society going? Charles Reich, the author, speaks of the United States, but in discussing the book it looks like he could be speaking about the old Europe as well."

Kloster says that from reading the book he can understand what a serious condition all societies are in. To change that condition we have to change our attitude toward money, our fellow human beings and life in general. Knut Utstein Kloster is not a pessimist. Rather he is a great optimist and also has the spirit of reformation.

Tracing a pyramid on a piece of paper he showed me a type of organizational structure. "See how far the top is from the base? It is the same thing in many industries. The owner and the executives are on the top and the employees are on the bottom. This cannot go on this way, from a human standpoint and also an economical standpoint. What social benefit has an industry where few give orders and everyone else has to obey them? The direction has to be very firm from the top, certainly, but then we have to squash the pyramid so that the distance between the top and the base is diminished so that employees can have more responsibility."

Is this a product of fantasy or vision? "Maybe," Kloster said. "But something is certain; things have to change and be done in a new way or else it will be bad for Americans, Europeans and everyone else."

He knows he is criticized. In Norway, some consider him a dangerous socialist, others a terrible capitalist. In the meantime, somebody else compares him to Joan of Arc, the Saint of Orleans. "Yes, Yes, Yes," Kloster commented, smiling, but not happy with it.***

Before the interviewer left, Kloster asked him very seriously, "Do you think we are doing something good, taking people on cruises?"

The question has haunted Knut for many years.

Rx for Tourism's 'Cultural Disparity'

A year before that interview in Genoa, *The New York Times* then travel editor, Paul J.C. Friedlander, wrote an article (December 6, 1970) entitled "Rx for Tourism's 'Cultural Disparity.'" The article described an early effort on the part of Kloster and NCL to close the gap between tourists and peoples and cultures they visit. Friedlander defined "cultural disparity" as "what happens when an affluent tourist who steps off a big airplane or luxury cruise liner, looks at the local shopkeeper, the waiter or chauffeur but doesn't really see him; when he talks at the locals he happens to brush against in some commercial context but never communicates or really talks *with* them. The disorientation works equally the other way when the local sees the visitor as a parasite to be fleeced or given as fast a back of the hand as possible — or, in extremes, as an evil not completely necessary."

The New York Times article is about the "New Experiences" program which Kloster instituted in 1970 for passengers sailing on NCL's *M/S STARWARD* from Miami to Jamaica. The basic idea behind the "New Experiences" program was to help interested passengers learn something about the island countries they were about to visit and to have genuine exchanges with local residents when they reached the island destination. To quote *The New York Times* article:

> The way the "New Experiences" program came about is as interesting as the program's potentialities. It started... as a directive from Oslo's Knut Utstein Kloster...who owns, along with a large Oslo-based fleet, the *M/S Starward* and her two sisters, the *M/S Sunward* and the *M/S Skyward*, and Norwegian Caribbean Lines. Kloster's directive raised the question of what the cruise line was doing for its passengers and for its destination countries. He had observed the cultural disparity that diminished what many passengers get out of their cruises, and he warned that unless something was done to bridge this obvious gap there might come a time when American tourists would not want to go to those destinations, and

when the locals and their governments might no longer welcome such visitors.

Kloster's challenge, as Friedlander observed, was "idealistic but also practical" because cruise lines must have destinations where their passengers are welcome. The ultimate goal of the program was to create the foundation for a positive attitude toward cruise passengers among the populations of the various islands visited and to enrich the experience for passengers.

In an interview with *Cruise Industry News* in 1999, "Knut Utstein Kloster — A Man of Vision", Knut explains his "idealistic but also practical" philosophy:

> In my book, being profitable means getting a good return on capital, defined as money, human resources and influence. The money side is obvious. You cannot talk about being profitable unless there is a healthy bottom line. But you also have the human resources side with all the people employed by the company. The return on this capital, broadly speaking, is reflected in the level of employee satisfaction and job performance. And then there is the influence side. By that I mean the company's potential for creating an environment in which it and the free enterprise concept will thrive — simply because people feel good about it.

The Shape of Things to Come

In 1972, Knut delivered a speech at the Convention of the Association of British Travel Agents, held in Vienna. The theme of the conference was "The Shape of Things to Come." In his speech, he got quickly to the point:

I could stand here today and describe for you in detail the physical shape of our future ships as I would envisage them...There would seem to be a certain degree of excitement in that, as the key to leadership in today's cruise industry is largely based on one's ability to maintain the newest, most modern fleet.

But I am not going to dwell much on that, because I don't believe that Newness itself will be the keynote of leadership in the future. I am convinced that our ability to meet the challenge of tomorrow will depend not so much on the physical shape of the ships, as on what we put into them.***

As I see it, the business of tourism, as all business, will ultimately have to be responsible to the society and ecology in which it exists.

This, of course, echoes the current mantra of corporate citizenship, where increasingly, corporations are interpreting the "bottom line" not only as their profit, but also, the manner in which employees are treated, and the impact of their businesses on the community and on the environment. All stakeholders must be included. Knut saw this from the very beginning of his career.

Trouble in Paradise

Despite the tremendous success of the new NCL venture in Miami, Knut's relationship with Ted Arison disintegrated when it was learned that Arison had been diverting, for his personal use, the passengers' prepaid cruise fares. Arison claimed that the money didn't belong to NCL until after the cruise had been concluded, but the contract he had signed with Klosters Rederi A/S expressly provided that all revenues were to be deposited into the Klosters Rederi account within 24 hours. That didn't happen.

The agency relationship between Arison and NCL ended and litigation ensued. It was a sad day for Knut; he had been close to Ted, his wife Lin, his son Mickey — and Ted's genius had most certainly contributed greatly to the success of the business. According to Knut, and as detailed in Kristoffer Garin's book, *Devils on the Deep Blue Sea*, after the breakup, Arison withheld NCL's passenger lists and millions of dollars in prepaid cruise fares. Ted used the monies to start his own company, Carnival Cruise Lines. Carnival grew to be the giant in the industry.

Although the enormously successful Arison later became well known for his community generosity and civic-mindedness, amends were never made with Knut or NCL. Ted Arison died in 2005. His son, Mickey, now runs the company. It's never too late to set things right.

CHAPTER TWO
On the Other Side of the Globe...

In some countries throughout the world in the early 70s, port congestion was a serious impediment to development. With virtual armadas of cargo ships lying at anchor outside clogged ports, vital materials — machinery, goods, foodstuffs and equipment of every type — were effectively blocked from entering these countries, seriously impeding the growth and development within those nations.

This was the situation in Saudi Arabia in the boom days of that nation's oil-spurred development. There was a great need for materials which were being shipped from all over the world, but, because of inadequately built port facilities, the ships could not dock to unload their cargoes. There were, for example, at the Port of Jeddah, queues of up to 90 ships which had to wait, often in excess of 100 days, to discharge cargoes. The result was a huge waste of resources, crew time and ship service, resulting in higher costs for transported goods, rapid inflation and a ripple effect that touched many other national economies. In a public statement made at the time, Knut said:

> Our firm has been turning its attention to the
> problems which different developing countries have
> in the disembarkment of cargoes. We found that large
> development projects have become paralyzed because
> building materials and equipment are not getting to
> their destination. Port operations in many places are
> bottlenecked by narrow streets and poor quality landing
> equipment in seaport towns. Although in most
> such countries the authorities make wholehearted efforts
> to find solutions to these problems, traffic in seaport
> towns has increased to the point where it exceeds the
> authorities' ability to cope. We decided to make contact
> with authorities in Saudi Arabia, and, after a period of
> planning, set up our project in Jeddah.

Kloster saw the port congestion problem as a "pilot project
of poetic simplicity." He purchased five laid-up U.S. Navy
LSTs (Landing Ship Tank) originally designed and built for
the United States Navy during World War II to serve as ocean-
going, amphibious ships for transporting and landing troops
and tanks on invasion beachheads. The idea was to unload the
cargo from ships at their anchorage, store the cargo onboard the
LSTs in semi-trailers which are then unloaded (landed) on the
beach where the cargo is then transported in the semi-trailers to
various inland destinations, bypassing the crowded port. From
ship at anchorage to destination, the cargo is handled once, in
the sense that the stowed medium (the semi-trailers) remain with
their load throughout the entire operation and until delivery.

Working with Resources and Industries Associates Group
(RIA) — a multi-country endeavor organized to pool talents and
resources to benefit developing nations — Kloster arranged for
conversion of the five LSTs. The main feature of the conversion
was the installation of long drop-ramps from the upper to the

lower deck. The existing ramps, intended for running tanks between decks, were not suitable for the semi-trailers to be used in this application. Each ship was to take approximately 50 semi-trailers onboard using both the upper and lower deck. The cargo would be loaded directly on to these semi-trailers which, in turn, would be trucked ashore through the ship's original

bow door and landing ramp arrangement. Another aspect of the conversion was to reinforce the upper decks with wood planking in order to provide a smooth surface for the trailers and redistribute their weight. Amazingly, the conversion of all five ships was accomplished in only two months' time.

Klosters Rederi A/S joined with a Saudi company to take charge of the harbor operations. The company was called Land-Sea Transport Company (LSTCO). Kloster's part of the operation involved unloading the cargo and getting it to the shore where a South Korean company took over for the land transport of the cargo. Knut chartered a passenger ship to accommodate the ships' officers and crew of over 1,200. His investment was $20 million. After only a few months, the LSTs had disembarked over 500,000 tons of cargo which was a very high percentage of all the total goods landing at Jeddah. The operation had the direct result of reducing the cost of consumer goods, flattening the inflation curve in that country, and serving as a prototype for solving port congestion problems in other developing countries.

Another byproduct of this successful turnkey prototype project was Knut's relationship with New York admiralty counsel, John S. Rogers, who helped coordinate the LSTCO project with Saudi authorities and who would later become Knut's partner in several other challenging ventures described in this book.

CHAPTER THREE
Make No Little Plans

"See first that the design is wise and just; that ascertained, pursue it resolutely."
— Shakespeare

In everything he does, Knut thinks outside the box. He thinks big and aims high. If he believes in something — if he sets his sights on accomplishing something — he will pursue it resolutely and not be deterred by the skepticism of others, nor by setbacks or delays. He is a man of strong convictions, with the courage to follow both his head — and his heart.

The cruise business in Miami took off like wildfire. Knut's vision spurred competition and before long, there were several cruise companies competing for what appeared to be — and has proven to be — an endless supply of cruise passengers.

Each new ship brought on line was a somewhat larger version of its predecessor, but there were no significant innovations, size or otherwise, and the largest ships accommodated only about 700-800 passengers.

After his disappointing breakup with Ted Arison in 1971, Knut continued at the helm of NCL. He had four very successful ships in operation but it became clear as the light of day to him that the industry was not meeting the rising expectations of cruise passengers nor capturing its full potential as an industry.

Land-based resorts offered many more options and amenities. Knut envisioned a floating resort that could compete with — and surpass — his land-based competition, adding the important element of a journey at sea. His cruise company rivals, on the other hand, proceeded with cautious optimism, choosing to expand and grow very gradually. The problem with building newer, bigger, better ships is that, in a sense, they undermine the existing fleet whose profits are needed to fund the new construction.

Kloster, always a maverick, was restless to break the mold. With his brilliant collaborator, naval architect Tage Wandborg, he considered all options — building a new ship or perhaps converting one of the great transatlantic ocean liners of the past. Many of these great ships had been laid up with the onslaught of air travel. Knut's ultimate choice, the *S/S FRANCE*, was viewed by rival cruise lines with utter disbelief; they saw it as "suicide" and didn't miss an opportunity to share their views and skepticism with the media.

The *S/S FRANCE* had been built in 1957 at a time when the era of transatlantic crossings was already losing ground to the air travel industry. By 1960, when the *S/S FRANCE* was launched, jet travel had taken over 70% of transatlantic travel. In 1962, after a five year construction period, during which time no expense had

27

been spared, the *S/S FRANCE* made her maiden voyage to New York. It was reported that, by the end of the decade, few travelers — less than 4% — preferred a five day sea voyage to a six hour flight. With the first oil crisis, it was clear that the *S/S FRANCE* could not survive economically and, after only twelve years in service, she was laid up. The golden age of transatlantic liners was over.

When Tage Wandborg first visited the *S/S FRANCE* in 1979 at Knut's request, she was laying alongside the appropriately named "Quay of Oblivion." Tage was taken aback by her beauty and majesty. "She was a masterpiece of marine engineering," he said. "The materials that went into her construction and engineering were the very best that money could buy. I felt awed by the sheer size of her hull and by her grace and elegance."

Tage spent two days on board the *S/S FRANCE* on that first visit. He returned shortly thereafter to Oslo and reported his

Knut and his wife, Trine Kloster, visit the S/S FRANCE for the first time.

observations to Knut who then asked how long it would take for Tage to say yes or no to the possibility of converting this transatlantic liner into a sophisticated cruise ship for the Caribbean. Tage asked for three weeks.

He hurried back to Le Havre, taking with him a team of experts. When the three weeks were up, he returned to Oslo and presented his conversion proposals to Knut and concluded the presentation with a resounding, "Yes, it can be done!"

Knut asked Tage to return to the ship with his team to work out complete documentation and invite shipyards to bid on the conversion. In the meantime, Knut started negotiations for the purchase of the ship. The vessel was acquired by Klosters Rederi A/S, under the NCL banner, and renamed *S/S NORWAY*. A German yard was selected for the momentous conversion.

However, when the vessel was ready to leave the port of Le Havre, to be towed to Bremerhaven, the French Workers Union protested vehemently that *S/S FRANCE* — proud symbol of the nation's maritime heritage — should leave the country. Thousands of people blocked the bridge which had to be opened to permit the vessel to be freed from her "Quay of Oblivion," where she has been kept in seclusion for the previous five years. Ultimately, the police were able to clear the bridge and

Members of the French Workers Union initially tried to block the bridge to prevent the S/S FRANCE from leaving the country.

S/S FRANCE bid adieu to her homeland. It has been reliably reported to this author that Kloster's fair treatment of his crews, and verification of this to French labor unions, played a role in resolving the difficult controversy.

Having been built for transatlantic crossings, the *S/S FRANCE* was a closed-in vessel to protect the interior from the ravages of the North Atlantic. Tage's job was to open her up to the Caribbean warmth and sunshine. As with the other transatlantic liners of her time, the *S/S FRANCE* was also a two-class ship. Kloster wanted the ship to be a classless ship where all the passengers could associate with one another and move about freely, without barriers. The one-time promenade decks were converted into two main thoroughfares, the Champs-Élysées and Fifth Avenue, which were later to be filled with shops, bars, cafés, restaurants, night clubs, galleries, etc.

When Knut went aboard the *S/S FRANCE* for the first time, he commented that "she seemed to be smiling at us; she seemed to know we had her best interests at heart." Knut had been given a 30 day option to purchase the ship and, within that time, based on Tage's report, he resolved to buy her. The price was $18 million. Even with the approximately $100 million refurbishment costs, it was a bargain and significantly less than the cost of a new ship of comparable size.

The *S/S NORWAY* was more than triple the size of any other ship serving the Caribbean cruise market. She was 66,000 tons, 1,035 feet (six city blocks) and accommodated 2,400 passengers. Instantly, it was the world's largest cruise ship and she held that record for over a decade.

Kloster's decision changed the industry overnight. The *S/S NORWAY* heralded a new generation of cruise ships that sought to combine many of the amenities of land-based resorts with the enchantment of a sea voyage. It was an entirely new and very exciting hospitality product. In addition to the traditional main dining rooms, the *S/S NORWAY* offered multiple restaurants, cafés, bars, lounges and a disco. The ship's huge theatre, which could accommodate 500 guests, soared three decks high and offered full-scale Broadway productions. Compared to conventional cruising, there were seemingly boundless opportunities for sport and fitness, shopping, recreation and entertainment.

The *S/S NORWAY* represented 40% of the total passenger capacity sailing year-round in the Caribbean. For all its skepticism at the announcement of the acquisition, the industry scurried to catch up.

In 1904, a tribute in words and pictures was published about the *S/S NORWAY*, still, at that time, the world's largest ship. Norwegian journalist, Alf G. Andersen, who contributed to the publication, had this to say about Knut:

A lot of people are surprised that Kloster has not adopted

the trappings and opinions commonly associated with the shipowning elite. He openly sympathizes with ideas and movements that spring from society's grassroots, so much so that in some quarters he is suspect for holding too controversial views. "I don't feel like a revolutionary," Kloster said. "I just follow my own guiding star, and it's up to other people to follow theirs. We all seek to do what we consider to be right and proper. I don't think stereotyped thinking should be allowed to replace an independent viewpoint and initiative."

Knut Utstein Kloster's Norwegian Caribbean Lines have built up a cruise empire. People from the world's industrial nations board the company's ships and are carried in comfort to countries and places where hunger is a fact of life. The company earns its livelihood in the border zone between affluence and abject poverty.

"Don't you find the contrast disquieting?" Mr. Andersen asked of Knut.

His answer: "I've never disguised the fact that I'm concerned with the impact of the cruise trade on Third World countries. I'm sure that it may safely be said that tourism helps to promote economic development, international understanding and community feeling. And there's no doubt that our cruises mean a great deal to the Caribbean countries visited by our ships and from which many of our crew members are recruited. But there's certainly another side to the coin, too. The collision of cultures that cruising involves provides considerable food for thought. And the long-term effects of the development cruising fosters are also open to question. But however one looks at it the fact remains that our cruise activity has generated a vast amount of employment."

The decision to buy and convert the *S/S FRANCE* required vision, courage and conviction. These are the same traits required of today's corporate and community leadership regardless of the nature of the endeavor.

Knut looked at the *S/S NORWAY*, with its diverse nationalities of officers, passengers and crew, as a little United Nations. There were between 25 and 30 different nations represented at all times in the crew of the ship. Add to that the multi-racial and multi-national backgrounds of the societies visited by the ship during her travels, and it's easy to see that the *S/S NORWAY* was truly a "Little United Nations" afloat. Knut contacted the UN to request permission to fly the UN flag on board the ship. Permission was granted by the (then) Secretary-General, Hon. Kurt Waldheim. The flag was hoisted at a special ceremony in 1981 when the ship visited her home port of Oslo. The ceremony was attended by His Majesty King Olav V of Norway, and Their Royal Highnesses, Crown Prince Harald and Crown Princess Sonja.

Knut's "Little United Nations" is a theme he has advanced for many years in other contexts. Whenever there is an opportunity to demonstrate that we are all in the 'same boat' and share responsibility for steering a just and sustainable course forward, Knut seizes it.

This desire, on Knut's part, to use his ships to bring people together and address problems of common concern, was to become a recurring theme in his life.

CHAPTER FOUR
Come, Let Us Build Us a City

A great city — a great solitude.
English proverb

With the success of the *S/S NORWAY*, Knut and Tage were convinced that the mega-ship concept was the way of the future and that the next leap would be to a size that liberated passenger accommodations from the confinement of the hull, thereby dramatically increasing the cubic space in the hull for other purposes. The result would be an island at sea, with three hotel towers rising boldly into the sunlight and sea air, offering vistas of the ship and the ocean from every guest room, and freeing up space in the hull for all the facilities and amenities which one would expect to find in a resort town or cultural center ashore, and much more! What they envisioned was, quite literally, a city-at-sea.

Knut dubbed the project "Phoenix" — named with the project's larger goals in mind. Phoenix is the ancient symbol of human aspiration toward universal good and of self-renewal.

Although one of the most extensive market surveys that had ever been commissioned in the travel industry confirmed the viability of the Phoenix concept, some of Knut's fellow executives at NCL disagreed with him, and they argued that a number of new conventional size ships would be needed to maintain NCL's share of the market. Moreover, at the time, NCL was preparing to go public and some board members felt that such a revolutionary project in the presentation of the company would be unwise. Too risky. NCL, then the most popular cruise line in the world (thanks mostly to the *S/S NORWAY*), ultimately decided not to pursue the Phoenix project. Knut recalls the decision-making process:

> At a board meeting in Miami, when the company's strategy was being discussed, I asked NCL's (then) Senior VP of Sales and Marketing what he would go for in a newbuilding program if the choice was between Phoenix and three conventional newbuildings with the same total capacity. He chose Phoenix. When I asked him why, he said, "Because I know I can fill the Phoenix to capacity in the first three years, at least — without any advertising." He expressed confidence that the ship's uniqueness, appeal, even celebrity as the world's largest ship would provide all the promotion needed to fill the ship.

But it wasn't to be. Knut decided to part ways with the company he had founded; he gave up his NCL leadership positions and bought out the Phoenix project, to be developed by him as a stand-alone venture. He saw the Phoenix project as the future of the industry and a maximization of its true potential, not only as a traditional cruise product but also as an American

Floating city of the future: a 5' x 6' oil painting by the American artist, Robert T. McCall, renowned for his space art and particularly his six-story mural at the National Air & Space Museum commemorating man's historic landing on the moon.

flag coastwise destination (see Chapter Five) and as a way to capitalize on the hospitality industry in emerging economies, particularly China (see Chapter Eleven). One of the qualities that Knut has exhibited throughout his life is the ability to stay the course, to have faith in his convictions, to remain undeterred in pursuing his objectives, however difficult.

World City Corporation was formed in Oslo and New York to develop the project. Knut and his New York partner, John S. Rogers, whom he had met in Saudi Arabia on the LSTCO port decongestion project (Chapter Two), came up with the name "World City" because it best described what they envisioned for life on board the city-ship and the larger goals to be achieved

through its realization. It is borrowed from, among others, the
works of Lewis Mumford who wrote extensively about urban
civilization. In his seminal work, *The City in History*, Mumford
uses the example of the medieval city as the basis for the "ideal
city" where the best and most vital human talents and resources
are brought together and integrated — the 'cosmopolitan' ideal.
This is what Knut and John Rogers envisioned for Phoenix and
the city-ship was thereafter known as *PHOENIX WORLD CITY*.
Tage Wandborg set about to convert the vision into a design
that would shape the future of the industry — in both size and
concept.

At the same time, World City Foundation was also
established. Its goals were to promote sustainable development,
environmental protection and international understanding, as
well as to fund programs and initiatives that foster leadership,
citizenship, corporate and social responsibility, business ethics,
scientific and technological achievement, global awareness, and
educational and cultural enrichment.

The idea was to steer a portion of the profits from the
operation of the ship to the foundation to support these larger
goals, and to use the ship itself to maximize its unique environment as a cross-cultural forum and global meeting place. The
harnessing of this major capital asset for the attainment of
shared international goals was part of a growing trend among
world business organizations to assume a more active role in
creating a healthier society and a more habitable planet.

When the late John J. McCloy[1] learned of Kloster's plans for
World City Foundation, he wrote:

---

[1] John J. McCloy was the Former High Commissioner for Germany; first President of the World
Bank; former Chairman of Chase Manhattan Bank; former Chairman of the Ford Foundation;
and former Hon. Chairman of the Foreign Relations Council.

It is an imperative that leaders in all fields make every effort to develop constructive interdependence among nations and improve the international decision-making process. The concept of introducing business leaders into the picture at this stage in world history is a very great one. What can I do to help?

Saburo Okita, Japan's former Foreign Minister and world-recognized economist and social planner, became a Senior Advisor to the Foundation and wrote:

This new endeavor has a very real opportunity to contribute significantly to the global community by helping to integrate national and international needs and interests in every field.

World City Foundation was to provide a vehicle — and a process — for activating a sense of world community and encouraging new dimensions of personal growth and development in all human cultures. The late Joseph Elliot Slater[2] became Chairman of the Foundation.

The goals of the Foundation are:

...to maximize *PHOENIX WORLD CITY'S* unique environment as a cross-cultural forum and global meeting place

---

[2] Joe Slater brought to the task a broad range of international experience in both the public and private sectors. He had served as Chief Economist of the Creole Petroleum Co., where he founded and directed the Creole Foundation; Program Officer in charge of the International Affairs Program of the Ford Foundation; President of the Salk Institute; and, for almost two decades, President of the Aspen Institute for Humanistic Studies.

...to demonstrate, in all of the Foundation's activities, that human potential is the greatest resource on Earth

...to articulate, in as many ways and for as many people as possible, a positive and achievable vision of the future

...to create a climate for the free exchange of ideas, the process of creativity and renewal, and the pursuit of excellence

...to foster and encourage a new generation of leadership and decision-making which is more human, more globally-oriented, and responsive to transnational problems and opportunities

...to bring together the best in ideas, talents and institutions to focus on new and more effective ways of looking at, thinking about and responding constructively to global issues and challenges and

...to engage the global business community and world leadership in a socially responsible, transnational mobilization of their productive endeavors...

... for the common good

John S. Rogers, Knut Kloster and Tage Wandborg present the PHOENIX WORLD CITY project.

The late Austrian political scientist and economist, Dr. Leopold Kohr, originator of the "small is beautiful" philosophy, often wrote about the ideal "human scale" community and dedicated a chapter to *PHOENIX WORLD CITY*, "by far the largest ship ever," in his book, *The Inner City*.

> How can I incorporate it in my smallness philosophy? As its name World City indicates, the point is that it is not so much the largest boat as the smallest planet; not the meaningless expanse of the world that includes a city, but a city that is a world in itself, "the universe in a little room," as Marlowe put it or, as Aristotle said in his definition of the ideal size of the state, "one that can be taken in at a single view." There will be no danger of the modern disease of inner city neglect and decay for it will be prevented from spilling over its 'walls' into the ocean, and the inner city as it always used to be will be the entire city once again. Phoenix arisen anew.

Kloster saw an opportunity to take the success, appeal and growth of the cruise industry and create an entirely new product that would attract a much larger segment of the travel and leisure market — and, importantly, contribute to public awareness and participation in issues larger than self. In addition to being a vacation paradise, offering every conceivable opportunity for guests to enjoy, entertain and enrich themselves, *PHOENIX WORLD CITY* also was designed to serve as a global forum for important corporate, educational, cultural and international events and activities, further enhancing its marketability. The objective was to bring together thought-leaders in business, government, science, education and public service, and to encourage them to use this congenial and stimulating environment to think creatively about common issues and global challenges.

Leopold Kohr had developed the concept of the Academic Inn© — a convivial place where people could gather and talk about the issues of the times. This concept derives from the tavern which was, with a church and a town hall, the center of the "inner city" activity in ancient human-scale towns and villages. Leopold kindly suggested that an Academic Inn© on board *PHOENIX WORLD CITY* would become an inviting place where visiting scholars, scientists, poets, authors, thought-leaders, professors, etc., could mingle with guests and, through lively conversation and the exchange of ideas, enrich the experience for all. And so it will be.

In an early description of the project, Knut wrote:

> *PHOENIX WORLD CITY* encompasses both a place
> and an ideal. As a place, it will be a unique world-class
> resort and global forum; as an ideal, it will symbolize the

process of international cooperation, understanding
and exchange. By creating a network of ideas, people,
organizations and institutions, we will enable
participants to take positive steps toward resolution of
differences, and toward improving the prospects for
peace and world order.

The city-ship concept is, of course, less of a technological
challenge today than when Knut and Tage first conceived of it.
This is because, in the meantime, the modular methodology for
building such a large ship has been developed and perfected,
and the most challenging technical issues have been addressed
and solved, many by World City's own design and engineering
team in collaboration with the world's leading technology
providers and regulatory agencies including the Norwegian
Maritime Directorate, Det Norsk Veritas, the United States
Coast Guard (USCG) and American Bureau of Shipping (ABS).
The industry has grown, exactly as Knut predicted, and, over
time, ships have become larger and larger and many of the
innovations developed in the context of the Phoenix project have
been emulated by other shipowners in their newbuild projects.

The Phoenix concept has already revolutionized the cruise
industry and the cruise experience. It was far ahead of its time
but its time has now come. At 265,000 tons, the city-ship is
the optimum size for capturing the full potential of the industry.
Almost two decades later, and after an investment of over
$60 million, the city-ship will be the world's largest and most
unique passenger vessel. A great deal of investment has gone
into the software side of the city-ship; the onboard experience
will be like no other place on earth. Also significant is the
combination of profit-making with a deeper purpose. Through
its operations, the city-ship will support worthwhile initiatives

in education, environment and development. When he first
learned of the World City project, Maurice Strong, former Under
Secretary-General of the United Nations and first Executive
Director of the United Nations Environment Programme, wrote:

> There is really nothing quite like it, and I have a strong
> and growing feeling that the World City project can
> become a global focal point for the kind of energies and
> initiatives required to ensure a more secure and hopeful
> future for the entire human family in the century ahead.

The Hon. Gro Harlem Brundtland, former Prime Minister
of Norway and Chairman of the UN World Commission on
Environment and Development, praised the initiative as
responsive to "the call for action" of the World Commission. She
emphasized that "private enterprise has a clear responsibility
for the future of the world" and that such future-oriented
commitments will "contribute to the widening of perspective
which is so urgently needed."

Peter V. Ueberroth, well-known for his superb organization
of the 1984 Olympics and as U.S. Baseball Commissioner, is
less known for his expertise in the leisure travel business. Peter
founded a travel business in 1963 which became the second
largest in North America by 1980 when he sold it to the late
Curt Carlson, of Carlson Companies, the Minnesota-based
hospitality powerhouse. Peter served as a director of both World
City Corporation and World City Foundation and had this to say
about the World City project:

> It is my expectation that *PHOENIX WORLD CITY* — as
> a unique resort and sea destination — will attract a
> major segment of the international traveling public in

its varied leisure, conference, business and educational pursuits. As a global forum and international business and cultural center, the range of World City's objectives — beyond travel and leisure — will match the physical magnitude of the project and will represent an important advance in the resort development and travel industries. *PHOENIX WORLD CITY* is, in my opinion, only a beginning, only the first in a new generation of floating resorts which will revolutionize the cruise and travel industry in the years ahead. Its potential for profitability is formidable.

The city-ship, at 265,000 GRT, was designed to a size and capacity that can amply accommodate 5,600 guests (6,200, including children), as well as a crew of 2,600. It is slightly larger than a Nimitz-class aircraft carrier with a beam of 244 feet at the main deck and a length overall of 1,235 feet. In addition to the three distinctive hotel towers, the ship houses an array of facilities including over 50,000 square feet of dedicated meeting, conference and exhibition space, a 2,000-seat theatre and concert hall. Executives, meeting attendees and seminar participants will have support 24/7 in the ship's business and communications center. There will be a multiplex cinema, sports arena, spa and fitness center, hospital, and wellness clinic. For art enthusiasts, the ship will boast a world-class arts center affiliated with a major land-based arts institution offering rotating exhibits from around the world. A television broadcast studio and media center will ensure that the ship's cultural, educational, philanthropic and business activities are shared with millions ashore, leveraging their impact. There are several exciting nightclubs being planned, including a 350-seat cabaret which will host popular bands, soloists, and comedians. As at any great resort, there will be numerous indoor and outdoor

Port within a ship: Massive stern doors in the city-ship open to reveal a large Kloster Marina which is home port to four 400-passenger high-speed day cruisers which can transport passengers to and from ports-of-call and other destinations.

pools, lovely gardens, parks and promenades.

Guests may choose to dine in any of the ship's nineteen restaurants, featuring a wide range of cuisines and an ambiance for any mood, budget or occasion. There will be dozens of bars, bistros and cafes, numerous public rooms, the world's largest seagoing casino, a library, specialty galleries, classrooms, art and music studios, game rooms, a children's playhouse, a kennel for visiting pets, a teen center with a Kids Only Cafe© and over thirty interesting one-of-a-kind shops and boutiques.

The size of the "city-at-sea" will provide an uncrowded sense of spaciousness and freedom notwithstanding the large number of guests which the vessel was designed to accommodate. A great city — a great solitude.

With a draft of only ten meters, the city-ship will be able to dock at all major ports-of-call but has also been designed to achieve convenient and highly efficient embarkation and disembarkation, whether alongside or at anchor. A unique feature of the ship design is a marina situated inside the hull and accessed through a large entrance in the stern of the vessel. The marina will be served by four 400-passenger day cruisers that can shuttle guests to and from various destinations within a 50 mile radius of the Mother ship. With this flexibility, no port is too small, no destination is inaccessible.

One aspect of the World City concept which particularly separates it from and elevates it above other travel, vacation and cruise experiences is the quality and range of onboard programs, events and activities to be offered. The underlying premise is that relaxation and leisure are enhanced by purposeful activity; that curiosity, creativity and spontaneity thrive in a congenial and relaxed environment; and that understanding and cooperation result as much when people relax and socialize together as when they work and plan together — and even more so when they do both.

For individual visitors and families, *PHOENIX WORLD CITY* will represent the opportunity to gain knowledge and perspective, to share experiences, and to be exposed to new ideas and higher goals. For executives, managers, and administrators, it is the chance to sharpen skills and learn new ones, to deepen their awareness of and sensitivity to global concerns, to rub elbows with their peers in diverse fields of endeavor, and to search for new and better directions. For world leaders, decision-makers, planners, problem-solvers, teachers, artists, writers and scientists, World City is fertile ground in which important seeds can be planted, nurtured and cross-fertilized. In sum, Knut's aim is to create an open and independent cultural and intellectual forum where creativity and new thinking can flourish. Utopia? No, but an opportunity to participate, contribute and feel energized.

In fact, what has just been described is, in many ways, what the World Economic Forum ("Davos") and the Aspen Institute have become for corporate and world leaders. Kloster's idea is to include the leisure traveling public and conference attendees in that process, and to help them use their vacation time or business meetings in a more productive, personally fulfilling and meaningful way.

The city-ship was designed to compete successfully as a cruise product and to also attract two larger markets, the general leisure travel market and the meeting and convention market. As Kloster predicted and pioneered, the trend in the cruise industry shows increasing popularity for larger ships, which are destinations in and of themselves, and shorter itineraries closer to home. Extensive market research confirms that the city-ship concept will attract a significant share of the current cruise market because of the uniqueness of the vessel, the diversity of activities offered and the extensive facilities, services and amenities available.

A major U.S. market, also of growing significance in Europe and Asia, is the business and professional convention and conference market. The World City ship is designed to have particular appeal for international non-profit associations, organizations and membership groups whose purposes are business, educational, cultural or scientific in nature. Because of the extended facilities required for even a medium-sized convention, conference or symposium, by comparison with the limited facilities available on even the larger ships, this enormous market will be drawn to the uniqueness of the city-ship environment which has the ability to keep the conference attendees together, to furnish thousands of comparable guest rooms and suites, and to provide a broader diversity of activities for accompanying spouses and family members, as well as boundless opportunities for recreation, entertainment, wellness and learning.

A part of the World City ship's identity is distinctively a corporate identity, and to maximize the value of the experience for corporate participants, World City developed a subscription program whereby 300 of the world's leading corporations are offered an opportunity to lease a corporate suite in the ship's exclusive center hotel tower for a period of five years with renewal rights for an additional five year period. The program is called the "World Class Corporate 300" and it will enable corporate participants to book conference facilities, to help shape the content of executive seminars and other executive programs, and to participate in decisions about World City Foundation's philanthropic activities and grants, leveraging them with their own grant-making when and as they deem appropriate.

Most significantly, World Class Corporate 300 subscriptions provide a financing device which enables the company to use the subscription proceeds, as they are earned from members' use of the ship, to take back equity and reduce debt. This financing scenario greatly enhances the project's ability to increase the quality of onboard programs, improve guest satisfaction and increase the bottom line. At the same time, it provides the means for supporting the company's larger goals and grant-making activities. Again, it is Knut's "2 + 2 = 5" *take* on life.

PHOENIX WORLD CITY — *The environment and the common good*

It has been Knut's objective from the start that, insofar as it is technically and commercially feasible, the city-ship is to be built and operated in a manner that meets the highest attainable standards of environmental responsibility and serves a higher purpose. World City has worked with participating corporations and governmental agencies to develop and utilize the latest environmentally-sound methods of construction, paying special attention to use of materials, work methods and commitment to innovation. A similar policy has been adopted in connection with the city-ship's operation. The ship's recycling and water treatment programs will ensure that absolutely no refuse or polluted liquids are discharged into the ocean. The ship's use of GE gas turbines, which utilize a higher grade fuel, will reduce exhaust emissions to levels far below those created by diesel engines which power most currently operating cruise ships. The ship's main engines will operate at the lowest fuel consumption per passenger of any powered commercial ship. Solar energy and other forms of alternative and renewable energy will be adopted for practical as well as demonstration use to the extent feasible.

Nevertheless, there is simply no way around it: *PHOENIX WORLD CITY* will consume fossil fuels. This has troubled Kloster from the very beginning. After incorporating every possible commercially available technology into the design and planned operation of the ship, Knut started thinking of what he could do to ultimately resolve this dilemma. One answer, given more time, is the use of one of the small, new, advanced atomic reactors. But this form of energy raises a new dilemma. Will the public trade long-held fears about nuclear power for a clean, green, zero-emission vacation or meeting at sea? This subject is a chapter of its own, Green Clean Global Village®, later on in the book. The World City team is also exploring the possible use of LNG (liquefied natural gas). While these options are being further developed, plans for the city-ship as the most environmentally responsible ship on the high seas continue.

"There are a number of reasons to build big, not the least is the ability to save 50% fuel per passenger and similar reductions in polluting waste," Kloster told a reporter from the Norwegian newspaper, *Dagens Næringsliv.* "In this sense, the city-ship is a ship of the future."

Kloster and his partners have reasoned that the resources utilized to create and operate the city-ship will represent a

definably minute fraction of the global resources utilized
annually for leisure purposes — but in its operation and in the
application of it revenues, *PHOENIX WORLD CITY* will represent
a major portion of resources devoted to global planning on the
part of the private sector and implementation of a sustainable
future.

"World City will be tapping into a huge leisure cash flow,"
Knut explains, "which will, *in any event*, be expended by the
populace and which will involve equivalent or greater resource
consumption. The major difference is that World City will apply
and leverage these financial and physical resources to achieve
significant objectives in changing the course of society in areas
directly affecting our future and the future of the planet."

"In real effect," he concludes, "the city-ship, over the 30 to
40 years of its life, will return to the earth many-fold what was
utilized for its creation and annual operation."

It is Knut's sincere hope that in addition to the influence of
the city-ship's programs and activities on passengers and the
public, the ship will fully regenerate and *recycle*, for the world's
benefit, the full dollar value of the resources which went into its
construction and ongoing operation on an average of once every
five years.

"The use of the city-ship, in conjunction with World City
Foundation and its grant-making initiatives," Knut explained,
"will leverage the effect into a series of outreach programs of
major international impact."

One of the Foundation's many programmatic ideas, for
example, is to annually recruit and train university students
from nations around the world in a certificated program, Our
Planetary Future©. Each year, a student from every nation in

the world will have passed through the six month program and then be sent back to his or her home country with a World City Foundation grant and supporting tools and materials to initiate school and university seminars and tutorials in cooperation with local institutions.

Onboard training programs for the ship's guests and meeting attendees will be one part of a continuous series of speakers, seminars and symposia. The value of these educational and training programs will be further leveraged by broad public dissemination via the ship's television and satellite broadcast studio. Printed materials resulting from these onboard programs will be packaged and distributed to educational institutions and organizations worldwide.

Just as the "world city" ideal historically represents a reaching out and gathering of the best in the world-*that-is*, Knut hopes that, when realized, his city-ship concept will have a positive impact on our common future and be a catalyst for broader participation in the process.

PHOENIX WORLD CITY — Safety and security

The design of the city-ship has set new standards in passenger safety. A revolutionary lifesaving craft and ship evacuation system was developed by Tage Wandborg and reviewed and accepted, in principle, by the Norwegian Maritime Directorate and Det Norske Veritas, the Norwegian classification society. The lifesaving craft and evacuation plan were also reviewed and accepted by the United States Coast Guard (USCG) and the American Bureau of Shipping (ABS).

Twenty large 400-passenger lifesaving craft (ten on each side of the vessel) provide convenient and efficient passenger evacuation in the event of an emergency. World City's lifesaving craft will be fully enclosed and ventilated, and provide for basic comforts with pantries and bathrooms. The lifesaving craft are at all times ready for instant boarding without any handling of equipment. They are suspended below the cantilevered overhang deck (main deck) so as to permit boarding from the deck below directly onto the craft through one of seven doors on each side of the enclosed craft, by contrast with conventional open lifeboats which must be swung out and then boarded over the ship's rail. This rapid, safe and convenient boarding feature is a factor in the projected ability to evacuate all guests and staff in 30 minutes or less. The ship will also have state-of-the art, high-speed boats for rescue operations. In addition, the ship will have a helicopter pad for emergency medical requirements.

A Navy-styled Safety Control Center on board will be staffed continuously. High pressure water curtains, fire alarm systems and fire fighting controls are located in this center. Basic fire indication systems are located throughout the ship and are supplemented by infrared fire detectors where additional safety is required. All public rooms will have sprinkler systems. The vessel will have nine fire zones.

World City's security system complies with, and far surpasses, all U.S. and international rules, regulations and procedures, including "new" proposals — many based on the safety and security features designed into the city-ship by Tage Wandborg and his team.

CHAPTER FIVE
Hands Across the Sea

The American Flagship Project

Although an idealist, Kloster is also a pragmatist and a realist. In his typical maverick and forward-looking style, and despite his Norwegian shipping roots and loyalties, he saw a dynamic business opportunity in a revival of an American Flag passenger ship industry. After all, up to 90% of the estimated $40 billion+ annual cruise revenues are generated by selling tickets to American passengers, and a vast majority of cruises sail out of U.S. ports. Knut therefore decided that his city-ship concept should be taken to America where the ship would be built and operated under the Stars & Stripes.

Building the ship in the U.S. was a decision that would involve innovation and considerable planning because the United States had not built a major passenger ship in over a half century. The Build America initiative would also set Kloster up against the powerful foreign-flag industry he himself had pioneered. It was a decision that would cost years of delay, millions of dollars in R&D, as well as considerable bureaucratic backtracking. But when the ship enters service, it will dramatically grow the industry, have an enormous impact on the U.S. economy, and set a new high standard for the hospitality and leisure/ travel sector — showing that pleasure and purpose, and profit and higher goals, can co-exist and prosper. Doing well by doing good.

It is possible, but not likely, that if Knut and his team on this side of the Atlantic had anticipated the true breadth of the American Flagship challenge and the enormous obstacles that would have to be overcome before contracting the world's largest ship in the United States, he *may* have had second thoughts. It is true, however, that neither Knut nor his U.S. colleagues anticipated how difficult it would be

1. **Alabama** — Heart of Dixie
2. **Alaska** — The Last Frontier
3. **Arizona** — Grand Canyon State
4. **Arkansas** — Land of Opportunity
5. **California** — Golden State
6. **Colorado** — Centennial State
7. **Connecticut** — Constitution State
8. **Delaware** — Diamond State
9. **Florida** — Sunshine State
10. **Georgia** — Peach State
11. **Hawaii** — Aloha State
12. **Idaho** — Gem State
13. **Illinois** — Prairie State
14. **Indiana** — Hoosier State
15. **Iowa** — Hawkeye State
16. **Kansas** — Sunflower State
17. **Kentucky** — Bluegrass State
18. **Louisiana** — Pelican State
19. **Maine** — Pine Tree State
20. **Maryland** — Old Line State
21. **Massachusetts** — Bay State
22. **Michigan** — Wolverine State
23. **Minnesota** — Land of 10,000 Lakes
24. **Mississippi** — Magnolia State
25. **Missouri** — Show Me State
26. **Montana** — Treasure State
27. **Nebraska** — Cornhusker State
28. **Nevada** — Silver State
29. **New Hampshire** — Granite State
30. **New Jersey** — Garden State
31. **New Mexico** — Land of Enchantment
32. **New York** — Empire State
33. **North Carolina** — Tar Heel State
34. **North Dakota** — Sioux State
35. **Ohio** — Buckeye State
36. **Oklahoma** — Sooner State
37. **Oregon** — Beaver State
38. **Pennsylvania** — Keystone State
39. **Rhode Island** — Ocean State
40. **South Carolina** — Palmetto State
41. **South Dakota** — Coyote State
42. **Tennessee** — Volunteer State
43. **Texas** — Lone Star State
44. **Utah** — Beehive State
45. **Vermont** — Green Mountain State
46. **Virginia** — The Old Dominion
47. **Washington** — Evergreen State
48. **West Virginia** — Mountain State
49. **Wisconsin** — Badger State
50. **Wyoming** — Equality State

on the political front, or that the foreign-flag lobby would be so powerful in Washington to successfully and repeatedly delay the entry of an American flag venture from capturing a share of the booming and predominantly U.S.-based cruise market.

There is no need to dwell on the political aspects of all this because, again, Kristoffer Garin has covered it well in his excellent book, *Devils on the Deep Blue Sea,* particularly the chapter entitled *"Hiding in Plain Sight."*

Giving back — and other good reasons to build the prototype city-ship in the U.S.

Kloster's reasons for deciding to embark on the American flag initiative were, again, a mix of pragmatism, realism, vision, sentiment and opportunity. From the beginning, he recognized that the United States had welcomed the foreign-flag cruise industry to its shores, and those foreign-flag companies, including NCL, had made their fortunes as a result. Of course, the U.S. economy benefits from the foreign-flag cruise industry, but there is also a compelling opportunity for America to seize a share of this booming market that is operating, to a large extent, on its shores and collecting huge American dollar revenues from American passengers. With a U.S.-built ship, the United States would benefit from a rebirth of commercial passenger ship construction, reap enormous tax benefits and create thousands of new jobs.

In deciding to undertake the American Flagship project, Knut was well aware of the fact that because most of the passengers are American, the foreign-flag cruise industry had become one of the *top ten* contributors to the United States' record high trade deficit, along with *countries* such as Japan, Germany, Mexico and China. It was only a matter of time, he reasoned, before U.S. politicians and the taxpaying public would awaken to this disturbing reality and want to claim a piece of the pie.

The industry is huge and growing steadily. "There's enough business for everyone," Knut said. Even though only a very small percentage of the potential market has taken a cruise (less than 10%), the industry represents the fastest growing segment of the leisure travel industry. "The American Flagship project has enormous potential to benefit the industry as a whole, the American economy in particular, and the larger leisure travel industry in general," Knut argues.

Another reason why Knut decided on the American Flagship project was because, under the American flag, the city-ship could trade along America's coastline, visiting ports-of-call along the way, and enabling tremendous flexibility in term of the guests' length of stay. Under the U.S. Passenger Vessel Services Act (PVSA), coastwise trading is (theoretically) reserved to U.S.-built and U.S.-flagged [registered] vessels. Most maritime countries also have such cabotage laws to protect domestic trading. There are similar laws in the airline business.

With coastwise itineraries and the added flexibility provided by the city-ship's day cruisers, guests would be able to check in and check out at will, just as they do at any hotel or resort. This increases turnover which is where the profits are made in this highly competitive industry.

Kloster recognized that to attract first-time cruisers, the meeting and conference market, and the larger general leisure travel market, passengers must have greater flexibility in terms of length of stay. They should be able to come aboard for one day, two days, three days, or however long they wish. One of the drawbacks of a conventional cruise is the need to usually commit to a 7-9-day cruise and a "foreign" destination (although this is changing as the foreign-flag industry continues to erode U.S. cabotage laws, discussed below, and in more detail in Garin's book).

Kloster further realized that, as ships become ever larger, they will be, like *PHOENIX WORLD CITY*, destinations in and of themselves, and guests will increasingly choose the cruise experience as a way to just get away, to participate in a broad range of recreational, cultural and educational programs and activities, and enjoy an array of entertainment, shopping, dining and other pleasures without having to travel very far to get there and without having to commit to a long voyage or to visit an increasingly overcrowded Caribbean destination.

Recognizing that the city-ship was designed to also attract the meeting and conference market, it is important to position the ship where meeting attendees can easily get to it, and leave when they choose to leave (as opposed to when the ship returns to port). Under the American flag, the ship will trade, for example, from New York in the spring, summer and fall, and from Port Canaveral in the winter months, which, taken together, encompass 25 metropolitan areas and 12 of the nation's and the world's largest tourist destinations, attracting a population of 100 million Americans within an hour's drive of a place where they can get on or off the ship. Moreover, under U.S. law, only meetings conducted on American-flagged vessels are eligible for tax deductibility.

As the cruise pioneer and innovator, Kloster was also considering ways to circumvent the cyclical nature of the hospitality industry in general and the cruise industry in particular. All resorts and cruise lines experience varying degrees of seasonality which affect occupancy as well as room rates. The high season in a given market segment is usually only four months. In order to keep occupancy up year-round, cruise lines and hotel/resort operators commonly discount room rates or offer upgrades or other incentives to attract guests during the low season.

Under the American flag, the city-ship could be positioned to attract markets which have their peak seasons at different times of the year — accessing those markets in their respective peak seasons — *year round*. Knut recognized that this flexibility, available only on a coastwise domestic itinerary — reserved under law to U.S.-built, U.S.-flagged vessels — would enable the city-ship to maintain high season occupancy *and* room rates throughout the year.

With the end of the cold war, and a great deal of talk at the time on the part of U.S. politicians of "downsizing" the navy and converting to dual-use (military and commercial) technologies, Kloster and his U.S. partners anticipated that they would be welcomed by the major U.S. defense-oriented shipyards with open arms. But, as it developed, these shipyards were not keen to take on commercial projects where margins — compared to military projects — are minimal and risks are much greater.

Understanding Title XI — The Merchant Marine Act, 1936, as Amended

Another motivating factor relating to U.S. construction is the availability of low-interest, long-term government loan guarantees for shipowners with economically sound projects who agree to build their ships in the United States. The loan guarantee program is called Title XI. The Title XI program is administered by the United States Maritime Administration (MARAD). Its stated purpose is to place shipowners on a par with large corporations in financing ship construction for sound commercial market opportunities.[3] The program accomplishes this by providing shipowners with favorable amortization periods (up to 25 years) and lower interest rates made possible by a federal guarantee of the privately placed debt instruments, and imposing economic soundness as a strict prerequisite for project approval. Ship owning is necessarily capital intensive, and, historically, shipowners (with the exception of major oil companies) tend to be smaller, single-purpose companies (often single-ship companies) by comparison with large multi-asset corporations in other industrial and commercial fields. It was to offset this reality that Title XI was enacted. It was, of course, recognized that, in the aggregate, the maritime industry has a far-reaching national impact affecting a wide variety of supplier and service industries, as well as myriad port and coastal communities.

Nothing in the Merchant Marine Act contemplated use of Title XI as a subsidy to offset any lack of competitiveness in U.S. ship construction or price disparity with ships built in foreign

---

[3] To operate under an American flag and to qualify for federal loan guarantees, U.S.-built ships must be owned 75% by U.S. interests.

shipyards, nor was Title XI enacted as a means of advancing objectives such as maintenance of the defense or manufacturing industrial base or a maritime employment pool.

In recent years, however, both the common perception of the Title XI program — and frequently the de facto application of it — have deviated from its original purpose.[4] As a result of this mindset, Title XI has come to be regarded as a form of subsidy and, as such, has on occasion been utilized as a device for exercise of political influence, with expectable results in terms of occasional high-profile — and totally avoidable — defaults (such as the aborted Fore River Shipyard modernization [Quincy, MA] and the American Classic Voyages' Hawaiian cruise ship default discussed below).

The Bush (George W) Administration zeroed funding of the Title XI program, deeming it a form of "corporate subsidy." World City America Inc., and many others, argued that this was the equivalent of throwing the baby out with the bathwater. A far better approach, it is argued, is to reform the program to eliminate unacceptable cost, risk and subsidy elements. Title XI is a financing tool that is essential to addressing major maritime market opportunities, including markets and revenues going by default to foreign companies and industries. The best possible example is the domination by foreign-flag interests of the booming $40 billion-a-year North American cruise industry which is supported primarily by U.S. passengers and U.S. dollar revenues. Title XI, properly administered, will provide the opportunity for the United States to harness that huge market

---

[4] On MARAD's web site, the list of the agency's "Programs & Initiatives," for example, places Title XI in the "Shipbuilding" category and refers to its purpose, in part, as "Supporting a shipbuilding industrial base for national security objectives." To the same erroneous effect, the New York Times (6/18/02) states: "The Maritime Administration's loan program is intended to support domestic shipyards…"

and channel a share of those revenues to economic growth, jobs, fiscal returns, trade balances, and other direct and indirect national benefits.

Knut reasoned that there was no better place for the Phoenix project to take hold than the United States of America. "As a nation with one of the longest coastlines and a seafaring tradition dating from its earliest origins, it just makes good common sense that the United States stakes its own claim in this U.S.-driven industry," he said.

In sum, going with U.S. construction and the American flag seemed to Knut to be a perfect opportunity all around and a great way to attract the additional new markets which the city-ship was designed to serve, while giving back to the citizens of a country that spurred the growth of this industry in the first place.

Knut fully recognized that a conventional-size cruise ship could not compete in the U.S. market as an American flag operation because, under the American flag, the owning company would have to pay U.S. corporate and payroll taxes and abide by generally more stringent (and therefore more costly) labor, safety and environmental "rules of the road."

Those competitive disadvantages would be offset by the city-ship's much larger size that permits more profit centers than on conventional cruise ships (i.e., greatly expanded shopping, dining, learning, gaming, spa, wellness and self-enrichment opportunities). The flexible, closer-to-home, coastwise itineraries, and the ability to check in and check out at will — *theoretically* possible only under a U.S.-flag operation — would greatly increase guest turnover and, therefore, the volume of discretionary spending.

To take advantage of this opportunity, Kloster entered into

The Hon. Helen Delich Bentley and Knut Utstein Kloster raise a glass to the American Flagship Project.

Knut announces his decision to take the Phoenix project to America.

a contract with John S. Rogers, a prominent New York admiralty attorney and longtime friend, under which a new U.S. corporation was formed to own and operate the prototype American flag vessel. It was agreed that the profits of the ship would be apportioned between Oslo, New York, and other U.S. shareholders.[5]

At the suggestion of Hon. Helen Delich Bentley, former Chairman of the U.S. Federal Maritime Commission and five-term member of The United States House of Representatives, the prototype American Flagship will be named *AMERICA WORLD CITY*. Thus, World City America Inc., World City Foundation (NY), and the American Flagship project were born.

A "National Collaborative" was formed to bring together dozens of major U.S. Fortune 500 Corporations which stood

---

[5] "The Title XI program enables applicants to obtain long-term financing on terms and conditions and at interest rates comparable to those available to large corporations. Funds secured by the obligation guarantees are borrowed in the private sector." Maritime Administration (MARAD) [60 Fed. Reg. 20592].

to benefit from the realization of an American-flag cruise ship industry — including GE, DuPont, AT&T, United Technologies, 3M, Alcoa, Delta Airlines, Caterpillar and many more.

As an independent, non-partisan, not-for-profit organization, The Build America Committee was created to promote the construction of the ship in the United States, and the former President of the Massachusetts Maritime Academy, Admiral John (Jack) Aylmer, was brought on as Executive Director. The objectives of the Committee were threefold:

- to energize the personal involvement of leaders from business, labor, government and media in support of America's bid to construct the city-ship in the United States and to promote operation of the ship under the American flag
- to maximize use of American technology, products and services from all fifty states in the building, outfitting and operation of the ship
- to provide a unique platform for a broader "Build America" initiative — one which will promote recognition of the resourcefulness and productivity inherent in the U.S. economy and serve as a catalyst for the renewal of America's industrial and commercial preeminence and its confidence as a nation

A "Build America Caucus" was formed on Capitol Hill, consisting of over a 120 members of Congress. The Build America Caucus was quick to recognize the enormous benefits to be derived from creation of an American flag cruise industry, including the following benefits that would flow from just the first in a series of next-generation city-ships:

structural steel/prefabricated stateroom panels and components/heat exchangers/tank systems/conveyors/tachometers/robotics/hydraulic and pneumatic equipment and systems/elevators/escalators/wastewater treatment/power generation, transmission and distribution/electrical installation/environmental systems/cables/cords/capacitators/hawsers/chains/

anchors/winches/windlasses/plumbing/heating/industrial safety/circuit boards/communications and navigation equipment/stabilizers/alarm, fire and sprinkler systems/plate glass/plexiglass/molded rubber/fiberglass/metal stampings/ventilation and air conditioning/industrial and commercial insulation/acoustical tiles/laundry equipment/automation systems/

meters/welding equipment/four 400-passenger highspeed daycruisers/twenty 400-passenger lifeboats/liferafts/rescue boats/lifesaving equipment/13 swimming pools/gangways/compressors/skylights/doors/windows/portholes/air, water and oil pollution prevention systems/laminates/sheet metal/precision metal fabrications/lockers/partitions/cabinets/

shelves/paints and plastic coatings/resins/propellers/shafts/ductwork and piping/relays/power switches/rudders/boat hoists/printing machinery/computer equipment/awnings/nuts/bolts/rivets/fasteners/steel tubing/manipulators/signage/gears/dehumidifiers/stairs/railings/cleaning equipment/turbines/transformers/gaskets/leak testing equipment/lasers/

control panels/weighing devices/batteries/marine compasses/clocks/recycling machinery/locks/industrial cleaning/beauty and barber equipment/furniture, fixtures and equipment for 2,800 guestrooms and 1,800 staff cabins including 8,000 beds/rugs/carpeting/chandeliers/tables/lamps/desks/television sets/VCRs/wall coverings and coatings/moldings/mirrors/faucets/telephones/curtains/draperies/bedspreads/fabrics/nightstands/shower curtains/mini bars/toilets/bathtubs/shower stalls/Jacuzzis/saunas/vanities/luggage racks/artwork/lighting fixtures/tiles/towel racks/counter

tops/lamp shades/sculpture/plants/planters/brass railings/track systems/entertainment units/armoires/dressers/veneers/cornices/wall panels/antiques/grill work/valances/coffee tables/pottery/hutches/sideboards/tapestries/wallites/sconces/consoles/sofas/blinds/stanchions/benches/chaises/murals/mosaics/Trompe L'Oeil/paintings/etchings/woodwork/signage/decorative surfaces/recreational, sports, exercise and fitness equipment/pianos/organs/luggage carriers/deck chairs/umbrellas/office machinery and equipment/dining tables and chairs/bar systems/trolleys/

banquettes/food processing equipment/furniture, fixtures and equipment for 92,000 square feet of dedicated convention and meeting space including 2,500 theatre seats/wall panels/banquet tables and chairs/podiums/communications, audio-visual and display systems/television broadcast studio/refrigerators/freezers/ovens/steamers/broilers/slicers/fire protection systems/utility distribution systems/work tables/floor grates/beverage dispensers/banquet carts/wine cellar/uniforms/towels/bed and table linen/china/glassware/tableware/cookware/cutlery/flags/ropes/medical equipment/life jackets/display cases

- $1.3 billion in construction, outfitting and supplies for U.S. companies
- over 10 million+ work hours for U.S. workers
- construction contracts valued at $500 million for the State of Florida
- $600 million in contracts for the Gulf States, including Louisiana and Mississippi; and $150 million in additional components, systems and supplies procured from every state in the union
- 2,600 onboard jobs for American officers, crew and hospitality staff, and thousands of jobs ashore
- over $4.5 billion in direct tax revenues over the life of a Title XI loan guarantee
- over $300 million in maintenance and repair contracts over the life of the ship operating on a coastwise itinerary out of Port Canaveral, Florida, in the winter months and New York in the spring, fall and summer

- an estimated annual impact on U.S. ports and coastal communities of over $500 million
- new levels of productivity and competitiveness for the U.S. maritime industry
- balance of trade improvements
- the psychological boost to public confidence from the nation embarking on an optimistic, forward-looking, entrepreneurial project, involving a cross section of American industry, to claim for Americans a role in a major high-profile market

A "Black Caucus" also was formed to help identify and capture opportunities for African-American businesses, large and small, and to create jobs in construction and hospitality for African-American citizens, including training programs for disadvantaged youth.

Mindful of the benefits of America's entry into the booming cruise sector, the United States Congress appropriated $15 million in the FY '93 Defense Appropriations Act for research and development funding for the American Flagship project. The Conference Report issued by Hon. Bob Livingston of Louisiana stated:

> Mr. Speaker, the conference report on H.R. 5504, the fiscal year 1993 Defense Appropriations Act, expressed the concern of the conferees over the general decline in the health of the American shipbuilding industry. As one of the provisions for defense conversion, the conferees directed that $15 million be utilized to establish and implement viable opportunities for conversion of the defense-oriented shipbuilding industry to market driven commercial production activities, help maintain the defense industrial base, and further the development

and maintenance of an adequate merchant marine. This
action was based on requests by leading U.S. shipyards,
corporations and other organizations, including the
American Bureau of Shipping, for applied research and
development funding to assist them in undertaking
construction in the United States of the largest passenger
ship in the world, *PHOENIX WORLD CITY*. The ship
would be the first passenger ship built in this country in
over 40 years, and it is projected to be the first of a fleet
of three such ships which will fly the American Flag and
operate, manned by American crews, on both coasts
and in Hawaii. While the impact of this national project
will be nationwide, a number of yards in my State and
along the Gulf Coast are already actively involved and
thousands of Louisiana shipyard workers could directly
benefit from the R&D program earmarked in H.R. 5504
and the possible construction work that could follow.
This project may have important economic significance
not only for the shipbuilding industry, but for
corporations across the Nation, for our merchant marine,
and for domestic ports and tourism. I believe that it was
the intention of the conferees that these funds be utilized
to help bring the American shipbuilding industry to a
point at which this major ship construction project can
be realized in U.S. shipyards and the industry thereby
positioned to address other commercial opportunities
that will surely follow.

In the first of many setbacks to be experienced, the American
Flagship project did not receive the FY '93 Defense Appropriations R&D funding. With a change in the administration from
President Bush to President Clinton, and political restructuring
common after a change of administration, the monies were
rolled over into President Clinton's Technology Reinvestment
Program (TRP). World City America, obviously disappointed,

nonetheless bounced back, putting together one of the most comprehensive teams in American history in support of its TRP proposal: "A National Shipbuilding Initiative: Phase Zero."

The team included the American Bureau of Shipping (ABS); the United States Navy; the Agile Manufacturing Enterprise Forum (AMEF) of the Iacocca Institute at Lehigh University; Concurrent Technologies Corporation; twelve of the nation's major defense and commercial shipyards, including Newport News, Avondale and Ingalls; Odense Steel Shipyard in Denmark (for 3D modeling); dozens of U.S. corporations including DuPont, AT&T, General Electric, ALCOA, 3M, Caterpillar and Westinghouse; six major universities including M.I.T., Clemson, Tufts, the University of Alabama and the University of New Orleans; and dozens of technology providers from across the country.

World City did not receive *any* of the TRP funding. As Kloster soon learned, the workings of the U.S. political system are much more complex and complicated than meet the eye. This was only the beginning of Knut's awakening to the reality of U.S. politics, pork and lobbying. Equally disappointing in terms of the potential benefits to the U.S. economy, the TRP "jobs" program did not turn out to be a successful "jobs" program either.

This is one of the greatest challenges of the Obama Administration — to insure that the billions invested in the stimulus program *actually create and save jobs*. It would be difficult, perhaps impossible, to find a better, lower risk, ready-to-go, privately developed, job-creating national project of the same scale and potential economic impact as the American Flagship project. In view of the sorry State of the Union in many manufacturing sectors, the American Flagship project would

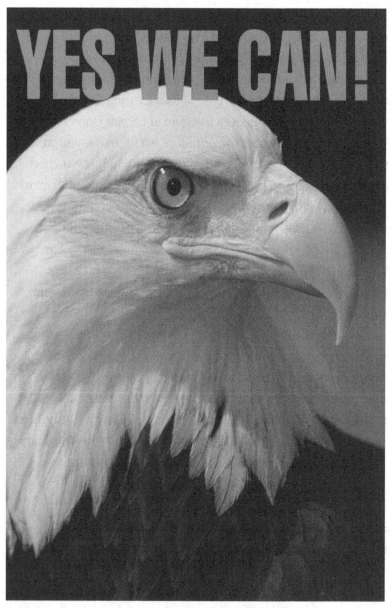

Although President Obama used the "YES WE CAN" slogan in his successful presidential campaign, World City distributed its YES WE CAN flyer to every member of Congress back in 2004 and views it as an appropriate "call to action" for all Americans and for all time.

provide the boost in morale and confidence needed to remind America: YES WE CAN.

The American Flagship Construction Program

World City carried on without any government support. An American technical team was assembled, including the former Commandant of the United States Coast Guard, Admiral J. William Kime, to direct all aspects of the ship's safety and compliance with U.S. Coast Guard regulations. Richard (Dick) Baumler, one of the United States' most experienced marine engineers, was brought in as Chief Engineer. Dick has had extensive dealings with and has held top executive positions at several of the major U.S. shipyards, including Newport News and NASSCO, and has served as Vice President for Ship

Left to right: Knut Kloster, Tage Wandborg, John Rogers, Dick Baumler and Jim Dolan (ABS), showing the ship model at a Society of Naval Architects and Marine Engineers (SNAME) conference.

Construction for Sealand.

World City chose Avondale Shipyard in Louisiana to prepare a ship specification and contract plans that were required for U.S. shipyard bid purposes, including all necessary Damage Stability, Fire Segregations, Structural Analysis and Critical System Analysis. As part of this process, Avondale was also to submit its own bid for construction of the ship at their facility.

Unfortunately, Avondale's bid proved to be uncompetitive, both in terms of price and schedule. A detailed analysis of the bid revealed that the principal cost drivers related to the construction and outfitting of the hotel components, an area in which Avondale (and all U.S. shipyards) lacked experience.

It was back to the drawing board.

Creating the Virtual Shipyard

A "virtual shipyard" replaces the vertical integration of a traditional yard with integration among multiple facilities and their suppliers and subcontractors. This approach supports and enhances current concepts of modular ship design and construction through electronic interface, uniform application of best practices, and responsiveness to market requirements. Work is allocated among participating entities according to core competencies.

Utilizing the "virtual shipyard" approach, World City America ultimately came up with a viable plan whereby the work would be divided among several construction entities, including a

[6] Centex has since become Balfour Beatty Construction, and some key members of the Centex team assigned to this project formed a new and highly successful entity, Moss & Associates. It is the intention of World City America Inc. to continue to focus on people and their core competencies in putting the final hotel construction team together.

major land-based hotel contractor, Centex Construction.[6]

In a 21st century application of the multi-yard and modular construction concepts conceived by Henry Kaiser to produce the famed fleet of Liberty Ships in World War II, World City America assembled a cross-section of U.S. commercial shipbuilding, offshore and general construction expertise, and resources for construction of the prototype city-ship.

Although the United States had not built a major passenger ship in over half a century, and despite widespread skepticism, Kloster and the team he had assembled for the American Flagship project, under John S. Rogers, had no doubt whatsoever that the United States of America had the industrial resources and expertise to accomplish the task of engineering and constructing the city-ship, and doing so on an internationally competitive basis.

Captain Warren Leback, former U.S. Maritime Administrator

(Seated) Bob Moss (left), then Chairman & CEO of Centex, with John S. Rogers, Chairman & CEO of World City America Inc. Standing are members of the build team with Tage Wandborg and visitors from a leading Finnish shipyard.

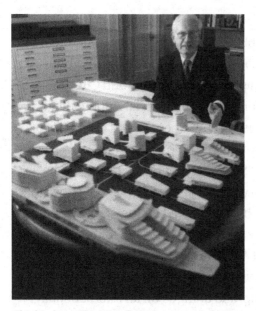

*Chief Architect Tage Wandborg demonstrates how
the modules of the ship's hull and superstructure
could be joined together.*

and also an advisor to World City, announced that "the innovative manner of constructing the city-ship will be as revolutionary as the product itself; the work will be undertaken by a consortium which will combine the skills and resources of the nation's shipbuilding industry with those of the highly competitive U.S. offshore and hotel construction industries."

Former United States Coast Guard Commandant, Admiral J. William Kime, became the Chairman of the American Flagship Construction Company (AFCC) that was formed to serve as prime contractor for the virtual shipyard consortium.

The hotel construction team worked for a year with Tage Wandborg, the United States Coast Guard and the American Bureau of Shipping and determined that it could build the superstructure and outfit the passenger accommodations on a competitive basis, to marine standards, both in terms of cost and schedule. In many respects, this was similar to what Centex and other successful hotel builders had been doing throughout the Caribbean and southern United States in building resorts

U.S. Maritime Administrator at the time, Captain Warren Leback, holds up model of the city-ship at MARAD headquarters in Washington, D.C.

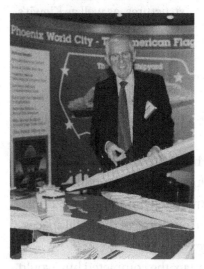

Chief Architect Tage Wandborg illustrates virtual shipyard concept at a Defense Manufacturing Conference.

to hurricane specification. Centex also worked with Wimberly, Allison, Tong & Goo [WAT&G] and Wilson & Associates — the interior architects and designers chosen by World City to handle the interior design of the city-ship — to research firesafe materials that could be used on board the ship, from wall panels, bathroom units, fabrics, carpeting, and furniture, fixtures and equipment (FF&E).

Under the innovative "virtual shipyard" construction concept, it was planned that the hull modules would be built in one or more commercial shipyards in the Gulf region and barged to an assembly site near Corpus Christi, Texas. Initially, VT Halter in Mississippi agreed to take the lead in terms of construction of the hull modules — 60 modules (43,200 long tons of steel). Halter indicated

Randall Wroblewski, who started out with World City as a Merchant Marine Academy Intern and who later earned an MBA in Finance, contributed enormously over the years to the project's business development, including assisting in the preparation of World City's Title XI application. Randy is seen here in World City's New York office with the company's voluminous Title XI application the day it was submitted to MARAD.

that it could produce these 60 pre-outfitted modules in 17 months, after appropriate planning, including possible delegation of work to one or more sister yards, such as Signal, Alabama Shipyard, and Bollinger. Kiewit Offshore Services was selected for the complex hull assembly and final outfitting based on its extensive experience in fabricating and assembling huge offshore structures, as well as Kiewit's outstanding safety record and on-time/on-budget performance.

Simultaneous with the hull construction, the plan called for the hotel modules to be constructed at a dedicated build site in Port Canaveral, Florida — the ship's future homeport. The hotel modules were designed and arranged to utilize required fire zone separations which would permit the complete outfitting of the hotel spaces in the modular stage prior to erection.

Ultimately, under this initial plan, the completed hull would be sailed around from Texas to Port Canaveral where the fully outfitted hotel modules would be skidded aboard. The ship's three deck "downtown" area would then be "stick built" on board, much like the construction of a mall ashore. The entire build cycle would take approximately 36 months and the total estimated cost was competitive, on both a per passenger and per ton basis, with leading passenger ship facilities in Europe.

Pro forma construction contracts were entered into and a comprehensive Title XI Loan Guarantee Application was prepared and submitted to the United States Maritime Administration (MARAD), costing several million dollars.

To meet MARAD requirements, World City America Inc. put together over $300 million in vendor financing and equity commitments from strategic partners including GE, Caterpillar, Siemens USA, and Grand Casinos. A leading investment banking firm, after studying the project, formally advised MARAD that it was confident it could raise whatever additional equity was required to complete the financing.

World City America retained Marsh Inc. — a world leader in risk management solutions — to review its construction plan. After a year-long study, including meetings with all participants, the United States Coast Guard, the American Bureau of Shipping and the United States Maritime Administration, Marsh offered World City a $1.3 billion Financial Protection Program which essentially guarantees the U.S. government and project investors that the ambitious and innovative "virtual shipyard" plan *will* succeed and that the city-ship will be built on time and on budget. This protection would be over and above normal construction bonding on the part of the build team.

World City America Inc. entered into a contract with Westin Hotels & Resorts to market and manage the ship and with Grand Casinos, Inc. to handle the gaming operations on board. World City selected Westin because it is one of the oldest and most

Left to right: Tage Wandborg, John Rogers, Stephanie Gallagher, Juergen Bartels [then Westin's Chairman and CEO] and Knut at announcement of World City's association with Westin Hotels & Resorts.

respected hospitality operators in the country and a leading upscale brand. At the time the deal was made with Grand Casinos, it was one of the largest and most successful gaming companies in the United States. Both Westin and Grand Casinos also made equity commitments.

After the management contract with Westin had been entered into, the hotel chain became part of Starwood Hotels and Resorts Worldwide, but maintained its own brand identity. The association with Starwood adds to Westin's marketing clout.

Lyle Berman, who was one of the founders of Grand Casinos, Inc., and the company's Chairman and CEO, later merged the company with Hilton Gaming to become Park Place Entertainment. Lyle did not include the World City contract in the merger and currently plans to operate the shipboard casino

under Lakes Gaming, Inc. Mr. Berman is a principal owner of
Lakes Gaming as well as its Chairman and CEO.

International Council of Cruise Lines (ICCL)[7] lobbies U.S. Congress

Although Knut anticipated *some* resistance from the foreign-
flag cruise industry to the American Flagship project, he and
John Rogers underestimated the opposition that would be
mounted by the industry when the Build America initiative was
announced.

It was more than the fact that the city-ship had the very real
potential to raise customer expectation beyond a level that the
existing foreign-flag fleet could hope to meet, though that was, of
course, a legitimate concern at the time. The foreign-flag cruise
industry had its own eyes on the advantages of a U.S. coastwise
itinerary and the resulting ability to offer shorter cruises to
increase turnover and revenues and to attract first-time cruisers.
But under the Passenger Vessel Services Act (PVSA), this is not
(theoretically) permissible.

The PVSA was enacted to ensure that American domestic
coastal water trade routes (i.e., transportation of passengers
from one U.S. port to another), like every other domestic
industry and means of transportation, are reserved to companies
that are subject to the full thrust of U.S. labor, tax, immigration,
environmental and workplace laws and standards.

The Secretary of Commerce applies a "domestic commerce"
test to PVSA, holding that a voyage on which passengers boarded

---

[7] ICCL has now merged with the Cruise Line International Association (CLIA), presumably to lower its lobbying profile.

a German ship in New York, traveled around the world visiting seventeen foreign ports and disembarked in San Francisco, was not "domestic commerce" coming within the prohibition of the Act. He reasoned that the disembarking of the passengers at San Francisco "was a mere incident" to a foreign voyage.

Camel's nose under the tent

Building on that rationale and subsequent Customs' rulings, foreign-flag cruise ships have worked the camel's nose under the tent, gradually eroding both the letter and spirit of the PVSA, as well as blocking one legislative proposal after another aimed at leveling the playing field or facilitating an American participation in this lucrative U.S.-based market.

The foreign-flag fleet now routinely conducts tourism voyages along the U.S. coastline, escaping the PVSA by including a non-U.S. port in the itinerary (e.g., a "fall foliage" itinerary from New York to multiple New England ports, ending in Halifax, Nova Scotia). It apparently has not yet occurred to the U.S. authorities that tourism, not transportation to the foreign port, is the commercial activity being engaged in and that such voyages obviously constitute "domestic commerce" in competition with American travel and hospitality industries.

Having, figuratively, gotten their nose under the tent, the foreign-flag cruise fleet now regularly sails up and down America's east and west coastlines, in Hawaii, and in Alaska, having only to add a foreign port to theoretically legitimize the activity. For example, using the "foreign port" rationalization, a number of cruise lines are offering year-round Hawaiian itineraries which call at four major Hawaiian islands, offering 23 Hawaiian shore excursions, and escaping the reach of the PVSA under U.S. Customs' interpretations by sailing to and calling for a few hours (if that) at the sparsely populated Fanning Island in the Republic of Kiribati. Similarly, ships trade out of San Francisco, Los Angeles, and San Diego by calling for a few hours (if that) at Ensenada, Mexico, and multi-port Alaskan cruises are offered by calling at Vancouver.

But the foreign-flag cruise industry would rather not be bound, at all, with the need to continue the pretense of "foreign travel" or be required to add that foreign port-of-call to many of their otherwise domestic itineraries. It has, for a long time, been a top priority of the well-funded foreign-flag cruise industry lobby to get the PVSA changed or repealed. The cruise lines deny this while continuing to use their powerful lobbying clout, and that of various ports currently benefiting from the cruise industry, to make steady headway on this objective in Washington.

Bob Dickinson, the former President of Carnival Cruise Lines, basically conceded that the cruise lines are taking a back seat in the battle, solely for appearance's sake:

> The cruise industry has been, by design, a bit of a bystander
> on this particular issue, only because we sense that… this is
> one that we're not going to win on our own. The port cities
> and port states have far more political clout than we do.
> They're the ones who are leading the fight.[8]

In a *Time Magazine*[9] interview, Dickinson also conceded the point that the cruise lines are not in the transportation business at all, but rather in direct competition with U.S. hotels, resorts and

[8] Source: *Journal of Commerce*, April 19, 1996
[9] *Time Magazine*, June 1997

vacation destinations:

> At the mass end of the market, however, cruise ships
> are entering an era when they must compete with land
> resorts in terms of price, entertainment and amenities.
> 'We see ourselves as a vacation business, rather than a
> cruise business,' says Dickinson, and he acknowledges
> that his competition increasingly is Las Vegas and Disney.

In a news release from Royal Caribbean some years ago,
announcing the construction of one of its large new ships, it was
conceded that the ship would "boast meeting and conference
space rivaling or exceeding that of many land-based conference
facilities" and will be "a total vacation experience equal to —
perhaps even better than — the best land-based alternative."

An American flag entrant into the booming cruise market,
especially the world's largest cruise ship, was seen as a real threat
to the cruise lines' long-held (albeit denied) political objective
regarding domestic coastwise trading. World City America Inc.
found itself consumed in the double challenge of doing what
many in the cruise business said was impossible — building the
world's largest passenger ship in the United States which had not
built a major passenger ship in over half a century — and fighting
a rear guard attack by the foreign-flag cruise industry's lobbying
organization. The process was, at best, awkward for Knut, but
he never wavered in his steadfast conviction that what he was
trying to do would be good for the cruise industry, good for the
travelling public, good for the American economy and destined
to ultimately be a huge success which would be good for World
City's shareholders and strategic partners and for the company's
larger goals as well.

American Flagship "Campaign"

As Knut recognized when he decided that the prototype city-ship should be built in the United States and operated under the American flag, the foreign cruise fleet had become a leading contributor to America's record high trade deficit. Surprisingly, when World City America Inc. began its "Build America" campaign, most members of Congress mistakenly thought the cruise industry *was* an "American industry," paying U.S. corporate taxes, hiring Americans and bound by U.S. labor "rules of the road."

Nor were many legislators aware of the actual *size* of the industry which, by the mid-nineties, had greater revenues than the nation's entire annual motion picture box office, the gate of

Former Coast Guard Commandant, Admiral J. William Kime, and World City America Inc. Chairman and CEO, John S. Rogers, pose with the Clintons at the White House. On this occasion, John Rogers asked the First Lady if she would be the Godmother of the American Flagship. The former First Lady graciously accepted.

America's four largest professional sports, and the total revenues of all Walt Disney and Universal Studios theme parks *combined*.

Obviously, this was a major business opportunity for the U.S. maritime and hospitality industries. World City America Inc. and the National Collaborative of U.S. corporations it had enlisted began a widespread mail, media and advertising campaign to awaken Americans and their legislators to the fact that America should be capturing a share of this predominantly U.S. market for its economy, workers and state and federal tax coffers. Members of the National Collaborative wrote to the Administration and to Congress urging support for the American Flagship project.

In its letter of support, AT&T wrote:

> We applaud the diverse group of skilled American participants, both public and private, which has been assembled to implement this truly national project, and we assure you that AT&T will do its part to realize both the integrated virtual shipyard and a state-of-the-art passenger ship to once again carry the nation's flag in international competition.

GE sent this message to members of Congress who represented Districts in which GE has U.S. operations:

> General Electric Company, one of the world's leading manufacturers of marine electrical and power systems, regards the American Flagship project as a major breakthrough in the use of the oceans for leisure and for business, and is pleased to be a part of this revolution together with other leading U.S. corporations…Also noteworthy is the proposed use of gas turbines on the

ship which will help realize World City's objective of creating the most environmentally-friendly ship on the oceans.

Caterpillar's message to Congress and the Administration was right to the point:

> World City represents a major breakthrough for our country, our citizens and the economy…this effort recaptures an industry dominated by foreign-flag vessels through the deployment of U.S. technology.

The President of Massachusetts Maritime Academy wrote the Massachusetts delegation:

> Our highly trained and motivated graduates increasingly find themselves "on the beach" watching foreign ships and crews sail away with U.S. commerce and passengers. This state of affairs need not continue. America can be competitive in both ship construction and operation, demonstrated by the American Flagship project…the Massachusetts Maritime Academy has supported this project from the outset and is proud to have been the first of our nation's maritime academies to enter into a training arrangement for cadets to serve on the ship as part of its onboard training program.

The American Bureau of Shipping (ABS), which is the nation's ship classification society, wrote this:

> The American Flagship project now stands contract-ready with an innovative construction plan — involving a revolutionary "virtual shipyard" that will bring together the best and most competitive that America has to offer in the construction of an historic new ship. We at

> ABS firmly believe that this enterprise is not only of a
> magnitude to enlarge the imagination and energies of
> companies across America as well as agencies of the
> government, but will stand as a symbol of renewal — an
> American Flagship with which all Americans can identify.

In an announcement to the Society of Naval Architects and
Marine Engineers (SNAME) in November 1995, the United States
Coast Guard stated that "World City is one organization which is
currently doing it right… this type of partnership with the USCG
should be the rule rather than the exception."

World City published a series of flyers aimed at educating
the public and Congress. The campaign was an enormous
success which explains why over 120 Members of Congress and
many state governors signed on to the Build America Caucus.
Nonetheless, behind the scenes and with a powerful lobbying
budget, World City America Inc. often found itself fighting a
steep uphill battle in Washington. It became a game of "May I?"
Two steps forward, one step back, much of the time.

Why does the World City project need the government's
support anyway?

Because the foreign-flag cruise companies start out with
a huge competitive advantage, including ship construction
subsidies in European shipyards, foreign government
financing, cheap Third World labor, and the fact that the cruise
lines operate in the United States virtually free of any of the
encumbrances with which U.S. companies must contend, such
as state, corporate and payroll taxes, and American laws relating
to labor, safety and the environment.[10]

---

[10] Knut understands the economics argument on both sides of the issue and is quick to defend
the foreign-flag cruise industry's contribution to the American economy and also to point out
that the industry's safety record has been outstanding. Under Knut's leadership at NCL, safety
was certainly a paramount consideration.

In Kristoffer A. Garin's book, *The Devils on the Deep Blue Sea*, he calculates that if, for example, Wal-Mart was earning at Carnival's tax-free profit margins in 2003, it would have made an unheard of $65 *billion* in profits, compared with the $8 billion in income Wal-Mart reported in that year — and paid taxes on. It's far from a level playing field.

The only government assistance which the United States offers U.S. shipowners is the opportunity to apply for low interest, long-term loan guarantees (Title XI).

Misguided upstart steals the stage

The Title XI loan guarantee program is administered by the United States Maritime Administration (MARAD) which, at the time the American Flagship project was launched in the early 1990s, had little acquaintance with the cruise industry. Moreover, World City's Title XI application was the largest in history.

After World City America Inc. finally inched its way painfully through the MARAD Title XI review process — which took years and cost millions — a competing American-flag initiative entered the fray (dubbing itself "Project America," a copycat initiative to World City's long-planned and arduously developed "American Flagship project") with a plan to build two conventional size vessels in a defense-oriented shipyard, Ingalls at Pascagoula, Mississippi — the state and hometown of Senator Trent Lott, then Senate Majority Leader. Ingalls is the State's largest private employer.

Senator Lott had met with World City executives, Admiral Kime, and Honorable Helen Delich Bentley on several occasions,

had seen the merits of the American Flagship project, and
pledged his support, as did many other members of Congress on
both sides of the aisle.

World City had spent millions learning that U.S. defense-
oriented shipyards were not able to compete on a commercial
basis in passenger ship construction, or, perhaps did not wish
to do so. But by the time American Classic Voyages' "Project
America" surfaced with its plan, Ingalls decided to take on the
project. Senator Lott naturally supported — and pushed for —
Project America's Title XI application. Since American Classic
Voyages (ACV) planned to operate the ships exclusively in
Hawaii, Senator Inouye, the senior senator from that State, also
pushed for approval of Project America's application.

World City's extensive market studies had demonstrated that
to compete under the American flag with the foreign-flag cruise
industry, a highly differentiated product to attract much larger
markets than just the cruise market was required.

MARAD (i.e., the U.S. taxpayers) paid most of the $5 million
cost of a market study that showed that the projected ACV ships,
which were to operate in Hawaii, could not compete with the
low cost foreign-flag cruise industry. They *could not compete*
even after Congress took the unprecedented step of granting
the ships a pre-construction monopoly[11] for their projected
Hawaiian operation as a way to offset the reality confirmed by
the market study.

Almost overnight, comparatively speaking, a $1.4 billion Title
XI loan guarantee was approved for American Classic Voyages.
"Project America" was ill-fated from the start, not only because

[11] Since the United States cannot dictate the commerce of foreign nations, the monopoly only
applied to competition from any American flag vessels, meaning that World City's ships would
not be allowed to compete with "Project America" in Hawaiian waters, but, of course, the real
competition was the foreign-flag fleet.

of the decision to build the ships, including the complex hotel components, in a defense-oriented shipyard, but also because of the undistinguished conventional design, size and concept of the vessels themselves. However well-meaning, Congress tried to substitute legislation for the marketability of the Hawaiian-based project, but because of loopholes in the Passenger Vessel Services Act, ended up excluding only U.S.-flag competition. Even before the keel was laid for the first vessel, the foreign-flag fleet lined up to eat America's lunch, yet again, by introducing bigger, better, cheaper foreign-built ships with all their low-cost advantages into the Hawaiian domestic trade in direct unfettered competition with the American-flag operator.[12]

"Project America" unfortunately played out just as World City had predicted. Neither ship was completed and the American taxpayers reportedly lost approximately $500 million in the process. This fiasco gave the Title XI program a black eye that would take Congress years to forget. It was right for MARAD, albeit belatedly, to attempt to facilitate America's entry into the booming cruise sector to take advantage of America's own powerful and growing markets and to encourage introduction of commercial standards and competitive methodologies in American shipbuilding. But it was a mistake for MARAD to ignore the realities of the marketplace and to imagine that a conventional cruise ship built in a conventional manner by a defense-oriented shipyard with little commercial experience and *no* recent passenger ship experience, could ever be positioned to compete successfully with the entrenched, low-cost foreign-flag fleet.

On the contrary, and as World City America Inc. had been

---

[12] As part of the Congressionally granted monopoly to American Classic Voyages, the company was permitted, while the new ships were under construction, to bring in a foreign-built ship and operate it under the American flag — not any more successful than the construction side of the scheme and for the same reasons.

urging for years, there is a compelling and irresistible market-driven opportunity for the American flag and the American merchant marine in the construction and operation of the next generation of cruise ships to serve America's growing interest in cruising, in tourism and in meetings-at-sea. However, this opportunity can only be seized by an equally compelling and irresistible product and a common sense next-generation method for constructing it.

To face-off with the entrenched, heavily subsidized modern foreign-flag fleet of over 200 ships, operating on American shores free of U.S. corporate taxes and without having to hire American crews or abide by America's "rules of the road" in terms of immigration and workplace compliance, an American operator has to have a competitive 21st century build plan and a highly differentiated product. It doesn't take a Harvard MBA to know that anything less than that — anything conventional in size or concept — will simply not make the grade.

There is no way to legislate around a bad plan, an uncompetitive product or an uncompetitive production methodology. That is, unfortunately, exactly what MARAD and Congress did with respect to the American Classic Voyages' "Project America."

Staying the Course

"Don't argue about the difficulties. The difficulties will argue for themselves." — Winston Churchill

As a result of the American Classic Voyages' debacle, Congress and the Bush Administration turned a blind eye to Title XI and

In Turku, Finland, John Rogers and Dick Baumler (left) and Admiral Kime and Tage Wandborg (right) pose with Finnish shipyard executives during the yard's design review.

the prospects for an American flag cruise ship industry. It has taken years, but hopefully, with proper administration of the program and adherence to economic soundness criteria, this important tool for economic development can once again be put to use by the current Congress and Obama Administration without incurring cost or any unmanaged risk.

The Credit Reform Act of 1990

The Credit Reform Act (Public Law 101-508, 2 U.S.C. 661a) was enacted in the wake of massive loan defaults in the Savings and Loan (S&L) industry in the 1980s. Because these loans were backed by the government without corresponding appropriations to cover potential defaults, they contributed to the federal deficit beyond the budgetary control of Congressional appropriators. In order to place limits on the authority of federal agencies to make loans and loan guarantees, Sec. 504 of the Credit Reform Act provides that for all future loans and loan guarantees, there must be budget authority to cover their costs. In other words, moneys are appropriated to cover what is, in essence, an insurance policy against possible loan defaults. The cost, known as a "set-aside," is measured by a given agency's estimation of the risk involved.

World City America Inc. has proposed a generic amendment to — or language in — an appropriations bill which would permit voluntary contributions to supplement or substitute for federal funds in meeting the cost of a Title XI loan guarantee for a passenger ship project. There is precedent for such a provision, and the Congressional Budget Office (CBO) has ruled that such

Good friends and long-time collaborators, Tage and Knut.

an amendment is "budget neutral." It makes sense, particularly in tough economic times, that ways be found to reduce the burden on taxpayers without forfeiting available financing tools, such as Title XI, to facilitate America's entry into the booming cruise market.

In the case of the American Flagship project, the proposed amendment would enable World City America Inc. to raise or contribute the cost of a set-aside associated with a Title XI loan guarantee while the Marsh Financial Protection Program would eliminate all risk associated with the construction of the ship under its virtual shipyard plan and guarantee Uncle Sam and World City investors that the prototype ship will be built on time and on budget.

Current Status of the American Flagship Project

As of this writing, we are well into President Obama's first term in office and, despite seemingly irreconcilable differences between Democrats and Republicans in the 112th Congress, we are told that the U.S. economy is slowly recovering. However, most Americans and both political parties agree that unemployment is the major challenge facing our economy.

There is no shortage of talk or commitment on either side of the aisle or on the part of the Obama Administration on the subject of job creation. But with the federal debt at record and unsustainable levels, it is generally agreed that new jobs must come from the private sector. The role of government is to reduce unnecessary regulatory barriers and adopt proactive policies.

World City America has proposed reforms to the Title XI program that would transform the underperforming and disparaged program into a proactive instrument of economic growth. The interpretation and application of regulations governing Title XI vessel financing assistance have (a) failed to protect against avoidable risk and cost, and (b) needlessly created a barrier to the nation's ability to respond to major maritime market opportunities and create maritime projects of a magnitude and complexity most likely to contribute to job creation and economic growth — most significantly, claiming a share of the U.S.-driven North American cruise industry.

The practical common sense adjustments to the regulatory process that World City America has proposed are entirely within the existing authority and discretion of the Secretary of Transportation (i.e., the White House) and would (i) restore Title XI's function as an instrument for advancing economic, industrial, trade, fiscal and other policy objectives; (ii) maximize the benefits and minimize risk and cost; (iii) correct those aspects of the program's application that have caused Title XI to be criticized and sidelined as a "corporate subsidy"; and (iv) facilitate immediate access by American companies to market-driven commercial revenue streams in the tens of billions of dollars annually, including creation of a new American leisure travel/entertainment industry, currently generating over $40 billion in cruise sector revenues annually that have been heading overseas for decades.

A new opportunity emerges

In July of 2010, Northrop Grumman, then owner of Avondale Shipyard, announced that it would close the facility in 2013 and consolidate its Gulf Coast operations to improve efficiency and address the nationwide problem of excess shipbuilding capacity. The closure could result in the loss of over 4,000 jobs. Since the announcement, Northrop Grumman has spun-off its shipbuilding assets and a new company, Huntington Ingalls Industries, Inc. (HII), now owns and operates Newport

News, Ingalls, and Avondale. The Gulf Coast operations will be consolidated at Ingalls in Pascagoula, Mississippi, and HII has reiterated plans to close the Avondale facility in 2013 but also said that there's still time to consider other alternatives.[13]

While Avondale could not come up with a competitive price or schedule for construction of *AMERICA WORLD CITY* back in the 1990s, World City carefully analyzed the Avondale bid and concluded that the yard could build the *hull* on a cost-competitive basis. The stumbling block had been the city-ship's hotel components — 2,800 guestrooms and suites and literally millions of square feet of restaurants, shops, meeting & banquet rooms, TV studio, theatres, and vast entertainment, cultural and educational facilities. Avondale was later acquired by Litton and then merged with Northrop Grumman which invested over a hundred million dollars in yard improvements.

Although World City's plan to build the 60 hull modules at a small commercial yard in the Gulf, and to then barge the modules to Kiewit Offshore Services in Texas for assembly, was a workable plan, given the situation at the time, there is no doubt that it would be a far better approach to build the hull in one piece, at one facility, and that Avondale is ideal for this purpose.

World City is currently pursuing this exciting option. If it is feasible, thousands of jobs will be saved and many new jobs will be created. Avondale will be positioned to lead the nation into a new era of commercial shipbuilding prosperity — working with hotel contractors and interior architects, designers and suppliers — to at long last seize a share of the booming foreign-dominated, but U.S.-driven North American cruise industry.

Always the wise man, and with a long view, Knut sent me

---

[13] Associated Press, April 1, 2011

an email recently, bringing to my attention a few inspiring lines from the Canadian poet, novelist and songwriter, Leonard Cohen — lines which he thought could be applied to World City's long struggle and imminent prospects:

> Ring the bells that still can ring
> Forget your perfect offering
> There is a crack in everything
> That's how the light gets in
>
> — *Anthem, Leonard Cohen*

"Yes," he said, "there is a crack in everything — that's how our light gets in!"

Washington has failed to see the light so far, but in these difficult economic times — with unemployment at an unacceptable high level, and with the President and Congress focusing on job creation — the American Flagship project stands out as an ideal, private-sector developed, contract-ready opportunity that can be prudently and responsibly seized, here and now, or as Knut sees it, "now or never."

CHAPTER SIX
Listening to Gaia

Gaia* is the name given by the ancient Greeks to their goddess of Earth and is the root of words such as geography and geology. The Greeks looked at Gaia as a living being, the cultural equivalent of Mother Earth or Mother Nature. In modern times, this "living Earth" idea resonates with new meaning.

The Gaia Theory, developed by the renowned British scientist James Lovelock, proposes that the air, the oceans, the rocks, and all living organisms on Earth evolved together as a single, inseparable system. This system serves to keep our planet in balance and habitable. According to the Gaian theory, the Earth regulates itself, much the way our bodies unconsciously maintain temperature, heart rate and other vital functions.

Many scientists, environmentalists and spiritual leaders have embraced the Gaia Theory because it evokes a great sense of belonging to and caring for our natural world. The idea of Gaia gives us a better understanding of our planet's strengths and frailties by emphasizing that humankind and the Earth's

*Pronounced guy-yah

resources are inextricably linked. It helps put our environmental
concerns in a new perspective by approaching the Earth's ills
in much the same way we approach illness and disease in our
bodies — through prevention, treatment and cure.

GAIA the Viking ship

When he first learned of Jim Lovelock's work on the Gaia Theory,
Knut immediately embraced the concept. At that time, he was
co-sponsoring with the Norwegian Broadcasting Corporation
and the governments of Iceland and Norway, a millennial
celebration of Leif Eiriksson's[14] voyage to America, called
"Vinland Revisited." To reenact the voyage, Knut acquired an
exact replica of a one thousand-year-old Gogstad Viking ship,
described as "a poem carved in wood." She would be named
GAIA, after Mother Earth. The name had been suggested by
Iceland's then President, Vigdis Finnbogadottir, and Knut readily
endorsed the idea. "By choosing that name," he said, "we are
giving the voyage the right profile. Our mission simply is to
create a better understanding of what Gaia (Mother Earth) is all
about, and what needs to be done to take care of her."

Knut supported the Vinland Revisited project because, in his
own words:

> It touches the spirit of exploration and discovery, the
> basic sense of having to stake something, in the pursuit
> of important goals. The willingness to take risks. Simple
> as that. And that's a spirit we need more than ever in
> the world today, with the tremendous environmental

[14] This is the Norwegian spelling of the name.

challenges with which we are faced, and the deepening
gap between the rich and poor in our common present.

The purpose of the Viking ship voyage was clearly expressed in
the Icelandic/Norwegian Vinland Revisited Agreement: "Our
primary aim is to gain respect for the environment of which we
are only a part. After 1,000 years of discoveries, we still have
not learned to live in harmony with the planet and each other.
We have yet to discover our common future."

When interviewed on the subject, Knut added that he also
was supporting the project "because I am fond of my country
and proud of our history as a seafaring people. From the early
Viking voyages to our modern fishing and shipping industries,
the ocean has always been our best friend and — sometimes
— worst enemy. That's how it is in Iceland, too. We truly have
common roots going far back in our history and deep into the
ocean."

GAIA sailed from Norway to Iceland, Greenland,

Former President of Iceland, Vigdis Finnbogadottir, christens the Viking ship, GAIA.

Newfoundland, Boston, New York and, finally, Washington, D.C.

GAIA's "map" for the voyage was the "Declaration for a New Global Agenda" prepared by Worldwatch Institute whose mission is to "deliver the insights and ideas that empower decision makers to create an environmentally sustainable society that meets human needs." (www.worldwatch.org)

Worldwatch Institute focuses on 21st century challenges including climate change, resource degradation, population growth and poverty. Knut found the Worldwatch declaration thought-provoking and an appropriate mission for *GAIA's* voyage. It states, for example, that "the goal of the cold war was to get others to change their values and behavior, but winning the battle to save the planet depends on changing our own values and behavior."

In a speech he gave at the MIT Club of Boston upon *GAIA's*

GAIA passes a huge iceberg on her way to Greenland.

arrival there, Knut explained why he viewed the Worldwatch declaration as such an appropriate "map" for the Viking ship's mission:

> Over the course of history, our European forefathers have extended their dominance over new continents, cultures and natural resources. The discovery of America, the subjugation of the old Indian cultures, the slave trade and the colonization of the rest of the world were all stages in this expansion. While our wealth and technology ended mass poverty among our own people, others had to pay with their cultural traditions and their natural resources. Those of us who reaped the benefits of our forefathers' expansion are 60 times wealthier than the poorest of the lands we conquered.
>
> Today, we no longer have a new continent to which we can expand and no more civilizations to exploit. Still, expansion and economic growth continue to be the mainstay of our society — and now it is the environment itself that is made to suffer.
>
> — *Knut Utstein Kloster, September 16, 1991, MIT Club Boston*

The Worldwatch declaration stands for the proposition that the long-term improvement in the human condition is contingent upon substituting environmental sustainability for growth as the overriding goal of national economic policymaking and international development: an appropriate "map" and mission for *GAIA's* voyage.

When *GAIA* reached a port of call, her huge sail was lowered and, in its place, a large banner was raised. It read:

> **A Thousand Years Ago**…Europe and America were brought together by the Vikings.

Upon GAIA's arrival in New York, there was a ceremony at the South Street Seaport Museum. Seen here, left of podium, is Hon. Gro Harlem Brundtland, Knut at the podium and GAIA's Captain, Ragnar Thorseth, to the right.

> **Since then**…Our knowledge of the world has grown
> faster than our sense to take care of it.
> **Now**…we must set the right course ahead and open up a
> new era.

A roundtable discussion entitled "From Vinland to Mars: The Legacies of Explorations" was scheduled for the end of the voyage and to be held at the Smithsonian Air and Space Museum in Washington, D.C. With a thousand years of discoveries behind us, from the early Viking voyages through Columbus and other great seafarers, to our modern voyages in space, the conference was intended to query what past discoveries tell us about the course we must follow in the future to meet the environment and development challenges of our time.

When the Vinland Revisited journey ended in Washington,

D.C., Knut was asked: "Did we make it?" His answer:

> Well, Ragnar Thorseth, the ship's Captain, and his crew —
> and *GAIA* — certainly did! The voyage was indeed a risky
> venture in spite of all the modern equipment on board,
> but they took the risk and made it.
>
> What about the rest of us? The Norwegian Government,
> the Icelandic Government, the Norwegian Broadcasting
> Corporation, and World City Discovery — the four
> partners who signed the Vinland Revisited Agreement
> and its "Declaration of Purpose" — did we make it?
>
> From the point of view of commemorating Leif Eiriksson
> and the voyages of a thousand years ago, Vinland
> Revisited was undoubtedly a great success. Many
> people were involved and they deserve our heartfelt
> appreciation.

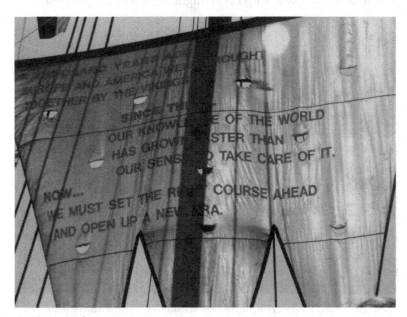

GAIA's mission banner

However, taking our declared purpose seriously — as we should — we must ask ourselves: To what extent did we accomplish the task of actually showing how important it is that the spirit of discovery in our modern times be aimed at shaping our common future?

This, of course, is a question to which there cannot be given a clear cut answer. But I think it is fair to say that in her special way, *GAIA* has touched the minds and hearts of thousands of people. If all of us use the memory of Vinland Revisited to re-shape our values and behavior, then we will have made it, too.

GAIA to Rio and the Earth Summit

Preparing for the Smithsonian conference, Knut began to think about how the Viking ship *GAIA* might serve a larger purpose

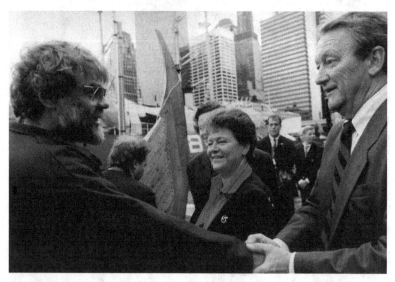

Norwegian Prime Minister, Hon. Gro Harlem Brundtland, watches with pride as Kloster congratulates GAIA's captain, Ragnar Thorseth.

than that for which she was initially commissioned. He was thinking a great deal about the upcoming United Nations Conference on Environment and Development (UNCED — "Earth Summit") planned for Rio de Janeiro in June of 1992. Working with John Rogers and the World City team in New York, and with Maurice Strong, the Secretary-General of the Conference, it was decided that, after Washington, *GAIA* would set her course for Rio. En route, she would gather thousands of messages of hope and concern from the world's children and young people and deliver those messages to world leaders attending the Earth Summit.

These were exhilarating times. To prepare for *GAIA's* voyage to Rio, contact was made with the then Executive Director of UNICEF, James R. Grant. It was decided that *GAIA* would sail to Rio under a UNICEF banner: KEEP THE PROMISE FOR A BETTER WORLD FOR ALL CHILDREN. The theme was anchored

in the World Declaration and Plan of Action from the World Summit for Children which had been held a year earlier at the UN.

Upon *GAIA's* arrival in New York, her new UNICEF banner was raised in a jubilant ceremony on the East River, outside the UN headquarters. Children from the UN School gathered along the pier to show their support, and about fifteen of the students came on board

Viking ship GAIA departs with her message of hope from United Nations Headquarters in New York.

the *SPIRIT OF NEW YORK*, which its owners had kindly donated for the ceremony, to participate in the celebration. The children read their own messages addressed to world leaders about their concern for the future of the planet and their own futures. A number of fire boats sprayed a shower of blessings on *GAIA* as she set sail for Washington, D.C., and then Rio de Janeiro and the 1992 Earth Summit.

In Washington, *GAIA* was greeted by dignitaries including Norway's Queen Sonja, Iceland's President Vigdis Finnbogadottir, and the U.S. President, George H.W. Bush. Hundreds of school children gathered to give their messages to *GAIA's* crew, and sang "We Are The World" as the Viking ship came into view.

After Washington, *GAIA* sailed to Port Canaveral where Jim Lovelock (founder of the Gaia Theory) and Apollo Astronaut, Jim Lovell, addressed the spirited crowd of hundreds as they gathered to bid *GAIA* farewell and fair seas on her journey to Rio.

From Port Canaveral, *GAIA* sailed to Cuba, Mexico, the Dominican Republic, Puerto Rico, Jamaica, Antigua, Guadeloupe, Martinique, St. Lucia, Trinidad, Venezuela, Guyana, Surinam and Manaus, the capitol city of the State of Amazonas in Brazil. Along her route, she gathered thousands of messages from children and young people for delivery by *GAIA's* crew to world leaders at the Earth Summit.

Gaia Camp in Amazonas

In cooperation with AFS Intercultural Program, Knut's Oslo-based World City Discovery brought together 150 students, aged 14-18 and representing 43 countries, to Gaia Camp Amazonas

Norway's Queen Sonja, and Iceland's President, Vigdis Finnbogadottir, await GAIA's arrival in Washington, D.C.

'92. The camp idea grew out of the wish to demonstrate how common concerns can be translated into positive action and also out of the wish to leave something behind of lasting value to commemorate *GAIA's* visit to the Amazon region.

The Amazon rainforest has come to stand as a prominent example of the dire global consequences that can result when development takes place

President G.H.W. Bush went aboard GAIA with two of his grandchildren to welcome GAIA to the nation's capitol.

at the expense of the environment. Brazilians have often had to bear the brunt of international criticism because of what is seen as a lackluster record in rainforest management. It was not surprising, therefore, that the City of Manaus, deep in the Amazon rainforest region, embraced the idea of Gaia Camp Amazonas. A piece of unimproved city property of 28 hectares would be transformed into a public park with nature trails and paths for the citizens of Manaus and visitors to the region to enjoy. The area would also serve as a "living laboratory," a rainforest microcosm, for school children and visitors to learn about animal and plant species indigenous to the region.

The initial planning and layout work for the park was done by volunteers from E.A.R.T.H., a program of the University of Costa Rica which is dedicated to teaching responsible natural resource management in the humid tropical regions of Latin America. The students' work at the camp was coordinated by local ecologists.

The students spent three weeks clearing away brush and trash, constructing paths and trails, and building steps, bridges and resting areas in the former wilderness, now named "Gaia Park." Signs were constructed which identified the flora and fauna that could be seen along the various trails. After a hard day's work at Gaia Park, campers returned to home base in Manaus where they participated in training seminars and discussion groups which focused on children, environment and development. Special emphasis was placed on the United Nations' *World Declaration on the Protection, Survival and Development of Children, and Plan of Action* for its implementation.

The idea at the heart of the camp, Knut said, "was that

Disney characters, Donald Duck, Mickey Mouse, and Chip and Dale, join World City America Inc.'s Chairman and CEO, John S. Rogers, at Port Canaveral to bid GAIA a safe voyage to Rio.

British scientist, James Lovelock, on board GAIA at Port Canaveral.

Grade school children visit GAIA en route to Rio.

students be given the information and training necessary to translate their environmental concerns into concrete action upon return to their home communities."

109

The Norwegian Prime Minister, Hon. Gro Harlem Brundtland, visited Gaia Park and planted a tree to commemorate the park's opening, which drew 2,000 visitors.

"The experience of these young people, living and working together for a common goal, made a deep impression on them," Knut said, "as illustrated by this excerpt from a statement written by one of the campers":

> During these days, I have sensed a deep unity, created by the unique mixture of so many cultures, backgrounds and personalities. Our main goal must be to revive our fundamental ability to love and appreciate the Earth, not only as the source of all material resources, but also for our psychological well-being.

During the last two days of camp, the students, who called themselves "Gaia Ambassadors," drafted their own messages of

Gaia Camp "ambassadors" cheer as GAIA departs from Manaus for Rio and the Earth Summit.

hope and concern about the environment and the future of the planet, to be carried by *GAIA's* crew to Rio and the Earth Summit. Six of the campers, representing six continents, joined *GAIA* for the last leg of the voyage from Manaus to Rio.

GAIALOGUE and Gaiafilm

BBC taped *GAIA's* exciting and challenging voyage from Norway to Washington and produced a video which aired on public television in Norway, Iceland, England and the United States. Since BBC's coverage ended in Washington, Knut put together an international film crew to cover the remainder of the *GAIA's* voyage. The end result was a spectacular and very moving film that was aired at the opening of the plenary session of the Earth Summit. With permission from the artists, the film featured the music of, among others, Lionel Richie and the late Michael Jackson ("We Are The World") and Bette Midler ("From a Distance").

Knut also arranged the publication and broad distribution of a journal, *GAIALOGUE*, to report on *GAIA's* activities and share photographs of the Viking ship's arrival in various ports-of-call and the festivities surrounding the visit. World City Discovery sent people ahead of *GAIA* so that school children could prepare their messages and local communities could organize educational and cultural events to take full advantage of *GAIA's* visit. Importantly, each issue of the *GAIALOGUE* had a '*Listening to Gaia*' article written by a prominent member of the world community. For example, Thor Heyerdahl, the noted explorer, wrote, in part:

> The message that *GAIA* carries from port to port — from the
> old world to the new, from the arctic world to the tropics

— is a non-political, or rather pan-political call for the protection of the natural environment, for peace, and for political and economic justice for the future generations of the whole world. In a vessel designed in ancient times with elegant lines that could harmonize and cooperate with the ocean waves, *GAIA* symbolically seeks to leap forward in time and leave behind a millennium of barbarism and wars, building a bridge to a 21st century of harmony and cooperation among young people with sound minds in sound bodies, in a sound environment.

We know that the indigenous inhabitants of the Americas lived in harmony with the forests, rivers, and mountains, and worshipped them. They had lived off the riches of the land and the waters for thousands and thousands of years before the first Europeans arrived in the Americas. Today we face the extraordinary challenge of reconciling the complexities and benefits of an industrial civilization with the inescapable requirement that we, too, must learn to live in harmony with Gaia and to responsibly manage the resources upon which this civilization depends. If we listen carefully, Mother Earth will tell us about the right path to the new world we wish to discover.

Norway's Prime Minister, Hon. Gro Harlem Brundtland, who had served as Chairman of the UN World Commission on Environment and Development, wrote one of the ʻ*Listening to Gaia*ʼ articles for the *GAIALOGUE*. Here are some excerpts:

> Our generation is gradually realizing something fundamentally new. The environment and development crisis will eventually affect us all, regardless of where we live and how affluent we seem to be.***
>
> Growing awareness and growing self-interest can produce the political momentum for the changes

needed. Poverty is where we must really start. To combat poverty, we need growth — particularly in the developing countries. We need a new kind of growth that is not based on overexploitation of natural resources. Sustainable development as defined by the World Commission on Environment and Development is a key concept for a new kind of growth. Democracy and public participation are essential for sustainable development. Consciousness raising and public participation are key prerequisites for global change.***

Our foremost responsibility to future generations is to ensure that there will be a world worth living in. The future generations are knocking on our door. The living conditions of our children and grandchildren will be determined now.***

Another '*Listening to Gaia*' article was written by Stephan Schmidheiny who, at the time, was the Chairman of the Business Council on Sustainable Development.[15] The Council was comprised of corporate leaders from around the world. In the years leading up to the 1992 Earth Summit, Mr. Schmidheiny was appointed by UNCED Secretary-General, Maurice Strong, to advise on business and industry. He called together 47 other chief executives who ran large companies such as DuPont, Volkswagon, Mitsubishi, Shell and Dow. The objective was to prove that environmental measures can be compatible with economic vitality. In 1992, the Council published *Changing Course: A Global Business Perspective on Development and the*

---

[15] Mr. Schmidheiny is honorary Chairman of the successor organization, the World Business council for Sustainable Development (WBCSD). The WBCSD gathers more than 170 of the most important global companies as members united by a common vision of sustainable development, based on three pillars: economic development, environmental balance and social progress. The council sets out to promote business leadership as a catalyzer for change towards sustainable development, based on eco-efficiency, innovation, and corporate social responsibility (www.wbcsd.org).

Earth (MIT Press), a 350-page report which was published in seven languages and provided an outline for sustainable development and a survey of the myriad ways industry and environmental interests mesh. In his *GAIALOGUE* article, referring to the *Changing Course* report, guest columnist Stephan Schmidheiny wrote:

> I do not mean to suggest for a moment that we have all the answers or agreed on every word. But we were able to agree on directions. For example:

> A free, open market best suits sustainable development because it maximizes innovation and equity of opportunity and can produce the economic growth needed to fund environmental management. But this market must be made to reflect environmental as well as economic truths. The price of a product or service must reflect the cost of either cleaning up or preventing the damage associated with that product or service…
> Just as there must be open markets nationally, so should there be internationally. Poor nations need to trade in order to develop, and need to develop in order to manage their environmental resources.***

> We had a lot to say to companies about using resources more effectively, preventing pollution, recycling, and setting up long-term commercial partnerships to transfer clean technology from those who have it to those who need it. We agreed on many other directions in which governments and companies might move, knowing we have to monitor progress and adjust the course along the way. Uncertainty as to destination must not prevent us from setting out.

> But we also agreed companies that move along the lines of sustainable development are not only serving the

needs of future generations, they are best serving the needs of their own stockholders and employees… the most eco-efficient companies will become the most valuable on the world's capital markets.

GAIALOGUE
GAIA TO RIO

Number 7, April 30, 1992

Gaia Park Dedicated in Manaus by Norwegian Prime Minister

GAIA to Rio...
a voyage of discovery
in pursuit of a new era...

to encourage
environmental responsibility
and equitable economic
development...

to learn how to live in
harmony with the earth...

to insure a healthier,
safer, and more secure
future in every
country in the world

Sailing Plan
One Month to Rio

March 18, 1992, was a special day for the people of Manaus, a city of 1.5 million citizens, located deep in the Amazon rainforest. That was the day Prime Minister Gro Harlem Brundtland of Norway arrived to formally open the Gaia Park. There she planted the first tree in what marked the beginning of an international reforestation relay. Brundtland is the chairman of the World Commission on Environment and Development, and considered by many an unofficial global minister for the environment.

It may seem odd to choose to plant trees in Manaus, which is already so rich in natural forest. But the Brazilian rainforest is under seige. It is being cut down at an alarming rate, and reforestation is necessary.

The Gaia Park is located in a jungle-like forest region of 27 hectares within the Manaus city limits. The area has long been eyed by developers who would like to make use of the property for housing and other projects. But instead of another development, Manaus will now have a public park, a sanctuary for all to enjoy. The area also will be a microcosm of the rainforest and a 'living laboratory' for school children and visitors to learn about animal and plant species indigenous to the region.

Manaus

Recife

Rio

Prime Minister Gro Harlem Brundtland at Gaia Park tree planting ceremony.

This issue of GAIALOGUE featured the dedication of Gaia Park by Norway's Prime Minister, Hon. Gro Harlem Brundtland.

GAIA's arrival in Rio marks the official opening of the Earth Summit and Global Forum

It was the culmination of a 12-month, 15,000 mile voyage. *GAIA* emerged out of a hot maze in Baia de Guanabara off Flamengo Beach in Rio de Janeiro against the dramatic backdrop of Sugar Loaf Mountain. Her arrival was the main attraction at the opening ceremony of '92 Global Forum, the gathering of non-government organizations devoted to environment and development which took place simultaneously with the Earth Summit. Thousands of people who had come from every corner of the world to participate in the Global Forum and Rio Conference were on the beach watching as *GAIA* slowly approached. Never before had a Viking ship visited these shores, and the excitement was palpable. Forget police barriers, never mind the waves and wet shoes, everyone wanted to witness this

GAIA arrives in Rio after her 12-month, 15,000 mile voyage.

historic landfall.

GAIA's Captain, Ragnar Thorseth, made his way ashore in the ship's zodiac in the company of the six Gaia Ambassadors, carrying dozens of mailbags containing thousands of messages gathered by *GAIA* on her long journey. The messages were addressed to world leaders attending Earth Summit and meant to serve as a reminder to "keep the promise" they had made two years before at the UN World Summit for Children.

A large stage had been set up on the beach and a group of distinguished guests were on hand: Hon. Gro Harlem Brundtland, Prime Minister of Norway; Mario Soares, President of Portugal; José Goldemberg, Environmental Minister of Brazil; Maurice Strong, UNCED Secretary-General; and Dr. Richard Jolly, Deputy Executive Director of UNICEF, to name a few. Actor Roger Moore, in his role as UNICEF spokesperson, hosted the ceremony. Knut was also present — and proud.

As Ragnar Thorseth and his Gaia Ambassadors began making their way through the crowd to deliver their messages, spectators, reporters and photographers crowded around the speakers' platform in a media frenzy. Speeches, song and dance lasted until long after sunset — a fitting opening to one of the most important conferences of the century.

Gaiaday

It was June 2, 1992, a Tuesday. In his statement, welcoming *GAIA* to Rio and the Earth Summit, Knut made the following observations:

> When the Viking ship *GAIA* set her sail in Norway a year

ago, she embarked on a long voyage that would finally bring her to the Earth Summit here in Rio. The purpose of it was simply to make a statement about our concern for the future. The world is like a big ship going in a dangerous direction. She now needs all the help she can get to move the rudder — and change the course — before it's too late.

During the voyage, *GAIA* has been in touch with thousands of people in many countries. She arrives in Rio now with a cargo of messages to the world leaders,

from children and young people. "Keep the promise," they say, "for a better world for all children."

If all these messages could be translated into an agenda for world leaders, we would probably get close to what is proposed in the *Human Development Report 1992*, recently published for the United Nations Development Program.***

That report reminds us that the gap between rich and poor nations has doubled during the past three decades. Restricted and unequal access to the world's financial, trade and labor markets cost developing nations and their poor populations $500 billion annually. That is nearly ten times what those countries receive in foreign aid.***

We who live in the rich nations must now understand that a fundamental improvement in the human

> condition worldwide is the key to a sound,
> environmentally safe future for our children and
> grandchildren.

A serious message, to be sure. That was, after all, the reason that over 30,000 people and leaders from every nation gathered in Rio for the Earth Summit and Global Forum.

But the festive spirit of the occasion also called for Knut to end his remarks on a lighter note. He suggested to the crowd that to constantly remind ourselves of the needs of Mother Nature and our responsibilities to her, we should name a day of the week in her honor. Since it was a Tuesday, the day of the week named after Tiw, a God of War, Knut suggested that Tuesday should be renamed Gaiaday and, as he stepped aside for the next speaker, he wished the crowd "Happy Gaiaday"!

Although Knut recognized that it wouldn't be easy to convince nations to change their calendars to rename one day of the week in honor of Mother Earth, he was (and remains) determined to promote the concept. To push the merits of his idea, Knut and his team had prepared two Gaiaday calendars, one for "grown-ups," to be distributed to world leaders at the Summit and corporate leaders around the world, and one for kids, to be distributed to schools and youth organizations.

The kids' version depicted some of the thousands of messages from children that had been gathered in communities along *GAIA's* 15,000 mile journey. The kids' calendar was named "Keep the Promise" and consisted of drawings, paintings, letters, and poems. On each page, there was also an appropriate quote from a world leader. For example:

> We must all seize this unique opportunity to advance

the peace and happiness of mankind by translating
into concrete actions the political will that has been so
evident during preparations for this Summit.

— *President Moussa Traoré, the Republic of Mali*

and

The Nicaraguan people are determined to strengthen
peace so that our children will be able to take their
rightful place in the future.

— *President Violeta Barrios de Chamorro, Nicaragua*

The "Keep the Promise" Gaiaday calendar was widely distributed
during the Earth Summit and also sent to schools of the children
who had visited *GAIA* along her 15,000 mile journey. The
"grown-up" Gaiaday calendar was named *"Changing Course"* in
honor of the forward thinkers who participated in the Business
Council for Sustainable Development (BCSD) and helped to
write their important report bearing the same title. In addition to
stunning photographs of *GAIA's* historic and purposeful voyage,
the *"Changing Course"* Gaiaday calendar featured quotes from
the BCSD report and gave monthly examples of what global
companies were doing to manage sustainable resource use
and change in business and global partnerships. The Gaiaday
calendar was a call to action, urging that a new course be set,
one filled with promise for humanity and the Earth. Thousands
of these calendars were distributed at Rio and sent to major
corporate and business leaders around the world following the
Summit.[16]

---

[16] Erling S. Lorentzen, a founding Member of the Business Council for Sustainable Development,
and then Chairman of Aracruz Celulose, an environmentally responsible Brazilian paper pulp
manufacturer, contributed to the cost of the Changing Course Gaiaday calendar and arranged
for its distribution to world leaders attending the summit.

Mission Accomplished — Children's Messages Delivered to World Leaders

From the canyons of Manhattan they came; from sprawling cities and tiny coastal villages up and down the Atlantic Coast; from tropical islands in the Caribbean to the humid rainforests of Amazonas. In paints, crayons and calligraphy; as books and posters, poems and models. There were thousands and thousands of them brought to the shoreline by children and young people who visited *GAIA* on her 15,000 mile journey to Rio and the Earth Summit.

They were messages of hope and concern about our common planet, our common future. Flying her UNICEF "Keep the Promise" banner, *GAIA* would act as messenger of the young; her mission was to assure that their messages be delivered to the world leaders gathering in Rio for the Earth Summit.

On June 14, 1992, *GAIA* kept her promise. At the opening ceremony of the Plenary Session on the final day of the Earth Summit, following an introduction by Conference Secretary-General, Maurice Strong, and the showing of the video on *GAIA's* year-long voyage, two young *GAIA* ambassadors of all the world's children mounted the dais and presented arms full of messages to President Fernando Collor of Brazil. President Collor received the messages most warmly and attentively on behalf of more than 100 heads of state who attended the historic summit.

Knut spent millions of dollars on the *GAIA* to Rio project — a voyage of discovery in a new era. Why? In his own words, "to encourage environmental responsibility and equitable economic development; to teach young people that it is possible to live in harmony with the Earth; to ensure a healthier, safer and more secure future for every child in the world; and to harness the energy, spirit and commitment of young people everywhere."

Maurice Strong, Secretary-General of the Conference, wrote the final *'Listening to Gaia'* column in the July 7, 1992 *GAIALOGUE*. Here are some excerpts from it:

> The growing awareness of the need for sustainable development is, of course, inextricably linked with the unprecedented political, economic and technological changes that are transforming our world into a single, interdependent planetary society. This interdependence is marked by the increasing globalization of the economy and the global and systemic nature of environmental problems. It comes at a time when the frontiers between East and West are fading, but the gap between rich and poor is widening.
>
> The gross imbalances that have been created by the concentration of economic growth in the industrialized countries and population growth in the developing countries, are at the center of the current dilemma.

UN Secretary-General Boutros Boutros-Ghali and UNCED Secretary-General Maurice Strong applaud the children's presentation of messages to Brazil's (then) President Collor.

Redressing these imbalances will be key to the future security of our planet in environmental and economic as well as traditional security terms. This will require fundamental changes in both our economic behavior and our international relations. Effecting these changes peacefully and cooperatively is, without doubt, the principal challenge of our time.

The industrialized countries must take the lead in effecting this transformation, for the unparalleled economic growth that has produced their wealth and power has also given rise to most of the major global environmental risks we face. Developing countries share these risks but are only at the early stages of the economic development to which they aspire, and their right to grow cannot be denied. But their growth will clearly add immensely to global environmental pressures and risks unless they, too, can make the transition to more sustainable modes of development. They can neither afford nor be expected to do this unless they have access to the additional financial resources and technologies they require to integrate the environmental dimension into their development.

Agreements on measures to meet these needs reached at the Earth Summit provide a promising starting point. Of special importance is a massive attack on the vicious circle of poverty in which so many millions of people are caught up, driving them to meet their immediate survival needs by destroying the environmental and resource base on which their future survival and well-being depends.***

No one meeting, even such an historic gathering as the Earth Summit, with over 100 Heads of State in attendance, could be expected to make all the changes necessary. But the Earth Summit has, I am

> confident, established the foundations for a wholly
> new global partnership based on common and shared
> responsibilities, one in which developing countries will
> have the incentive and the means to cooperate fully in
> protecting the global environment while meeting their
> needs and aspirations for economic growth.

It would be easy to get frustrated and lose hope, particularly when we see with what difficulty genuine change is fraught, but Knut doesn't see it that way. He is convinced that every journey begins with a single step, that every light lights the way, and that the 30,000 participants who gathered at Rio for the Global Forum and Earth Summit — as well as the thousands of children who entrusted their messages to *GAIA*, and the thousands more who were inspired by *GAIA's* mission — have not forgotten what is at stake or that they have personal and collective responsibility to implement the changes needed to build a better world for all children. "Each of us must follow our own heart," he says, "I feel good about my *GAIA* investments. To me, Tuesday will always be Gaiaday, in honor of Mother Earth."

CHAPTER SEVEN
Planet Earth at Ground Zero

The soul-shattering destruction of the twin towers at the World Trade Center in New York City on September 11, 2001, was heard and felt in every corner of the world, and will never be forgotten.

When Knut learned that the Lower Manhattan Development Corporation (LMDC) was organized to assist New York City in recovering from the terrorist attacks and ensuring the emergence of Lower Manhattan as a strong and vibrant community, he wished to contribute in some meaningful way. He knew that the centerpiece of the program was to create a permanent memorial remembering and honoring the thousands of innocent men, women and children lost in the terrorist attacks.

In 2002, the LMDC announced a design competition for a memorial that would honor the victims and recognize the endurance of those who survived, as well as the courage of those who risked their lives to save others:

> May the lives remembered, the deeds recognized, and
> the spirit reawakened be eternal beacons which reaffirm

respect for life, strengthen our resolve to preserve
freedom, and inspire an end to hatred, ignorance and
intolerance.

Knut was very moved by the challenge and discussed with Tage
Wandborg possible concepts for a fitting memorial at Ground
Zero. Knut felt the importance of bringing the world together
at this time of terrible loss and fear. He wanted to show the
interdependence of peoples and nations and solidarity. He
envisioned a huge globe as the centerpiece of the memorial,
because it would remind everyone that Planet Earth, like
the twin towers, is vulnerable and that each of us, and every
nation, must come together in search of peace, justice and
equality for all.

Tage wholeheartedly embraced the concept of the Globe
— of Planet Earth at Ground Zero — and designed it as a
breathtaking 750-foot wide big blue marble, reminiscent of
the view of Earth from outer space, a precious and fragile jewel
reflecting the sea and the sky. At night, the globe would be
illuminated and appear as a sparkling diamond from miles
around and from outer space. Inside Tage's huge globe was a
70-story atrium giving way on all sides to a rose sculpture in
honor of the victims. It was proposed that the globe would
stand on six elevator towers and float 150-feet above a beautiful
memorial plaza, without touching the footprints of the twin
towers.

Knut's idea for the Ground Zero Memorial, and Tage's design,
were intended to provoke the sentiment of Adlai E. Stevenson
in this excerpt from a speech to the UN Economic and Social
Council, Geneva, Switzerland (9 July 1965):

"We travel together, passengers on a little spaceship, dependent on its vulnerable reserves of air and soil, all committed, for our safety, to its security and peace. Preserved from annihilation only by the care, the work and the love we give our fragile craft."

— *Adlai E. Stevenson*

CHAPTER EIGHT
Creative Capitalism

Bill Gates uses the term "creative capitalism" to describe the notion that profit and social responsibility are not mutually exclusive and that capitalism can also improve the lives of those who have not traditionally benefited from modern market forces — i.e., the billion people on the planet who live on less than a dollar a day and do not have basic necessities such as access to clean water and electricity.

In an article written for *Time Magazine* (August 2008), Gates describes creative capitalism as "an attempt to stretch the reach of market forces so that more companies can benefit from doing work that makes more people better off." The article is supplemented with a number of excellent examples, such as Grameen Bank in Bangladesh which has disbursed more than $7 billion to over four million of the world's poor, of which 94% are women (98% of the loans have been repaid — a recovery rate higher than any other banking system); Sumitomo Chemical which shared technology with a Tanzanian textile company that has made millions of insecticide-treated mosquito nets (mosquito nets are crucial tools in the fight to eradicate malaria); and Vodaphone which bought a large stake in a cell phone company in Kenya that has found ways to serve the economic needs of low-income Kenyans and make a profit doing it.

Time Magazine also conducted a roundtable discussion on creative capitalism. John Mackey, founder and CEO of Whole Foods, was among the panelists. He prefers to use the phrase "conscious capitalism" — what he describes as a 21st century business paradigm that embraces the complex interdependencies of the multiple constituencies involved. This, in essence, is what Knut has been advocating for the past three decades. The interdependency and interconnectedness of all the stakeholders is the reality in which corporations exist today and, according to Mackey, "our economic and business theories need to evolve to reflect this truth."

Mackey says that the common perception about the purpose of business — i.e., to maximize profits — is a myth. "Most entrepreneurs do not start businesses in order to maximize profits." Referring to Bill Gates, Mackey said: "He had a passion for software; he wanted to put computers everywhere, he wanted to transform the world. That was the passion... that's not about maximizing profits, but it worked pretty well!"

Mackey argues that a transformation is needed in the way we think about business. "People want businesses to do good in the world. It's that simple." Conscious capitalism, as John Mackey sees it, and practices it, is a new social/political/ economical/environmental business model that encourages the entrepreneurial spirit for good:

> In my business experience, profits are best achieved
> by not making them the primary goal of the business.

Rather, long-term profits are the result of having a deeper
business purpose, great products, customer satisfaction,
employee happiness, excellent suppliers, community
and environmental responsibility — these are the keys to
maximizing long-term profits. The paradox of profits is
that, like happiness, they are best achieved by not aiming
directly for them.

(http://www.flowidealism.org/Downloads/JM-CC-1.pdf)

Economist Milton Friedman wrote that "there is one and only
one social responsibility of business — to use its resources and
engage in activities designed to increase profits so long as it
stays within the rules of the game, which is to say, engages in
open and free competition, without deception or fraud." Like
Knut, John Mackey disagrees. They, and many other enlightened
leaders, believe that corporations should try to create value for
all their constituencies. "From an investor's perspective," Mackey
argues, "the purpose of the business is to maximize profits. But
that's not the purpose of the other stakeholders — for customers,
employees, suppliers and the community. Each of those groups
will define the purpose of the business in terms of its own needs
and desires, and each perspective is valid and legitimate."
Mackey's business model is one that "more consciously works
for the common good."

That model is the one that Knut has embraced in his
businesses for many decades. It is encouraging that successful
business people, such as Bill Gates and John Mackey, have
helped put this topic on people's radar screens, and, most
importantly, are putting their money and brains to work on the
potential of capitalism to make the world a better place and
spread the benefits of the free market system.

In 1987, Knut gave a speech at the International Association of Independent Tanker Owners (INTERTANKO) annual meeting. Intertanko is a group of independent tanker owners who have as their goal to "ensure that the oil that keeps the world turning is shipped safely, responsibly and competitively."

In his speech, Knut said that he had been motivated to accept the invitation to speak, in part, by the fact that "no specific theme" for the speech had been suggested. He interpreted that to mean he could "talk freely" about what he sees as "perhaps the most fundamental of all our mutual interests today [i.e.] to promote free enterprise and create new business opportunities for the maritime industry by participating actively in the process of moving the world forward in the right direction."

Many of the things Knut said in that speech track the message Bill Gates gave in his *Time Magazine* article and in his January 2008 speech at the World Economic Forum, as well as John Mackey's public statements about "tapping into more powerful motivations than self-interest alone." Here are some relevant excerpts from Knut's 1987 speech:

> Our objectives as companies and as an industry should clearly continue to be as result-oriented as before in terms of bottom line profitability and return on invested capital. But our visions of the future must be expanded in scope.***

> No longer would it be adequate to say that our job is just to transport cargo from A to B. A new dimension would be added in our traditional evaluation of profitability. This kind of thinking is the way to position the whole maritime industry in the large, global picture. It results in strategies which are right, which strengthen the image of "free enterprise" as a constructive and socially

responsible force — and it gives us the opportunity to play an active part in shaping and, in the long run, gaining lasting benefit from — a well-balanced, equitable and sustainable economic growth worldwide, with international trade and transportation as the basis for our existence.***

The shipping industry is, by nature and tradition, the most internationally-oriented industry in the world. Now is the time when we should put ourselves in the driver's seat and place the concept of "free enterprise" in a value system which will be perceived by people everywhere — through our attitudes, actions and the way we conduct ourselves — as being good and meaningful.***

The task now is to define our global mission and set a new course which will strengthen our basis for making money and for meeting other objectives as well. From what I have said here already it will not come as a shocking surprise to you if I suggest that the maritime industry should take the high road and let its agenda focus on the role we could play as a major visionary pathfinder in the world. For example, at the next INTERTANKO Annual Meeting, it would be interesting to generate a well-prepared discussion on what the trend in supply and demand for tankers would be if an industry course is set for a more equitable distribution of energy in the world, as conceptually defined in the report from the UN Commission on Energy and Development. Or take the Law of the Sea — as a gateway to opportunities in undersea mining and farming which could generate new technical, transportation and other services. Or the United Nations Environmental Program (UNEP) with "Earthwatch" and the possibility of making our ships active participants in the process of protecting the environment.***

Great rewards in the way of new commercial
opportunities could be gained by expanding our vision,
our horizon, and our commitment to larger goals.

An article in the Norwegian paper *Dagens Næringsliv* in the early
1990s dubbed Knut the "Kind-hearted Capitalist." Again, we
see his forward-looking recognition that business has a role
beyond profit-making:

It is plain to see that Knut Utstein Kloster travels off the
beaten track…everyone agrees that Kloster is a man of
contradictions, a genuine combination of capitalist and
idealist, a wealthy and influential businessman who is
deeply concerned with the deplorable state of the world
— and who truly wants to do something about it.***

He sighs deeply and gazes out the window. The view is
wide and lovely from the offices of World City
Corporation in Ullern Alle. From here Kloster directs
a number of activities which he hopes will wed his
concern for environmental and developmental issues to
conducting business in a sensible way.***

Make no mistake, Kloster is still a businessman with
blind belief in the power of the market economy. "The
role of the market is to identify demands and fulfill
them. But is it up to the politicians to determine the
parameters? I believe the business community must play
a far more active role. Meanwhile, we must devise a more
meaningful way to measure real growth in our society:
A concept such as the gross national product makes no
sense because it doesn't include the future cost of today's
pollution and depletion of resources. We need some
sort of awakening — something that will foster a new
awareness and new attitudes."***

> Is Knut Utstein Kloster a giant Pooh Bear, a merchant of
> milk and honey with the seven seas as his Hundred Yard
> Forest? Or is he a man ahead of his time, a prototype for
> the humane and socially enlightened leader of the future?

The "awakening" and "new attitudes" to which Knut was
referring are seen today in leaders like Gates, Mackey, Google
founders Sergey Brin and Larry Page and many others.
Fortunately for the planet and for the free market system,
there are many more such visionaries and socially responsible
entrepreneurs today than when Knut was being labeled a "naïve
dreamer" for having such thoughts and convictions back in the
60s, 70s, 80s and even in the 90s.

The Role of Conscience

In 1991, the *Boston Globe* wrote an article about Knut, calling
him "the conscientious capitalist" and "one of Europe's most
successful proponents and defenders of free enterprise." The
article quotes Knut as saying that free enterprisers are "going
to have to promote new values that start taking care of Mother
Earth."

> Kloster doesn't claim to know the way out, nor does he
> see himself as the environmental crusader who will rally
> the forces. He maintains he's just a small addition to a
> burgeoning group of capitalists with a conscience.

Capitalism with a conscience is also described as "social
entrepreneurship," the practice of seeing profit-making as
only one element of success, with the company's impact on

customers, employees, the community and the environment as the other determiners of "success." It's clear to Knut that conscience plays a big role in how capitalism will be defined by the global community in the years to come.

In dictionaries, conscience is defined as 1) "the sense of what is right or wrong in one's conduct or motives, impelling one toward right action"; and 2) "the complex of ethical and moral principles that controls or inhibits the actions or thoughts of an individual."

In a homily defending the "The Rights of Conscience" given in 1995 in his homeland of Poland, the late Pope John Paul II described conscience as "man's most secret core, and his sanctuary." Deep within our conscience, he explains, we discover a law which we have not laid upon ourselves but which we must obey.

Our conscience is our inner guide, our "true north," and it also is our judge. Pope John Paul II reminded us that "to be a person of conscience means...working for what is good...it means courageously assuming responsibility for public affairs... being concerned for the common good and not closing our eyes to the misery and needs of our neighbor..."

Conscientious capitalism, then, is capitalism that integrates economic, social, environmental and other criteria; it considers such issues as climate change strategies, energy consumption, human resources development, knowledge management, technology sharing, stakeholder relations, and transparency and accountability in corporate governance.

Knut Utstein Kloster has, throughout his life, exemplified this caliber of corporate and global citizenship. He has "walked the talk" for decades — long before it became a popular subject which, still today, is more talk than walk for far too many corporations and corporate leaders.

In a speech that he gave to the Norwegian-American Chamber of Commerce in 1981, Knut spoke about "The challenge and conscience of a capitalist in today's society." I'm going to share much of that speech with you because I think it touches the heart and goes to the core of the subject:

> Since we have just finished an excellent meal, let's start with a story about a prominent Senator from Oregon who hosted a luncheon for his colleagues. At the plate which was served, his — I presume — somewhat startled guests around the table found just a tiny piece of meat and a very small potato, nothing else. In his welcoming speech the Senator told them that the purpose of serving such a meager meal was simply to show them — or remind them of — how much food the great majority of people in the world got every day to sustain their lives. I don't know if he also mentioned the fact that about 80,000 children die every day from starvation or malnutrition.

> The message here of course — in the context of our theme today — is clear: Since everything is relative in this world, each and every one of us being here today at the Waldorf Astoria is a super privileged capitalist as compared to the mother and the father of the child who is dying right now… and now… and now — every second, day in and day out, all year round. The clock is ticking off the painful hours, and deep down in the abstract part of our conscience we all feel guilty about it.

> As a business man, however, I am not supposed to regard this catastrophe as particularly relevant to what I am doing. My job is defined in terms of commercial activities, not in terms of saving the world and the

children who are dying. That is for the politicians to do. That's their work. They have been elected to deal with it — to solve all the big problems — poverty, starvation, violence, unemployment, the arms race, energy shortage, pollution — you name it. Thank God we have the politicians!***

Whenever people in the U.S. are polled on their attitudes toward institutions in the country, business ranks close to the bottom. It's no use moving backwards into the future, but if we talk about the multinational companies' impact on the world, it is difficult to push under the carpet the fact that the whole free enterprise concept in a global perspective very often is associated historically with exploitation and so-called "economic imperialism." Rightly or wrongly. And we are all in the same rich-country boat here, whether we like it or not.

Therefore, if we want the world to be a friendly open market for our products and services in the future, we must in my judgment challenge ourselves continuously — ideologically, philosophically and morally. We must define the nature of our business in terms and in a language which is understood and accepted, and we must conduct ourselves and our operations in a manner which can be respected widely.

For example: What do we mean by "free" enterprise? Perhaps we should begin to talk more about a *sound* enterprise system or a *healthy* enterprise system, because it can be free without being very healthy, but it cannot be healthy without a reasonable degree of freedom. It is like talking about *life* standard instead of living standard. You can have a good living standard without a good life standard, but you cannot have a good life standard without a reasonably good living standard. When it comes to our goals and business objectives, it is not adequate any more to just say that the name of the game is profit or to make money even when we talk about it off the record. Yes, we must have a reasonable financial return on the invested capital — that goes without saying — but what is capital? Money? Yes, but that is only part of it.

In his new bestseller, *The Third Wave*, Alvin Toffler has a chapter on "The Corporate Identity Crisis" where he talks about the "many bottom lines," or multiple bottom lines — social, environmental, informational, political and ethical bottom lines — all of them interconnected. He also talks about the concept of social reporting and the new language of accountability. Indeed, he says, accounting itself is on the edge of revolution and is about to explode out of its narrow economic terms of reference.

The Shell companies, for example, today list five overall corporate goals — only one of which is to achieve a "reasonable return on investment" — and specifically states that each of the five goals, economic and non-economic, must "carry the same weight" in corporate decision-making. The goal accounting method forces the companies to make their trans-economic objectives explicit, to specify time periods for their attainment, and to open this up to public review.***

The notion that you have to do well financially before you can do so-called "good" is fundamentally misleading. But it is a difficult process indeed for many reasons to implement effectively such goals — partly because they tend to challenge our deep-rooted, traditional attitudes.

In such a perspective it seems logical to say that a capitalist is someone who is in a position to decide how money, human resources and influence are being used for a common purpose.***

As business leaders we should begin to move ourselves more freely into the mainstream of society, and not just stay in our traditional boxes, in the same old conservative place, with low personal profiles so that nobody can see us. If the business community is suffering from a credibility gap in society, or if it is difficult for us to communicate our ideological message effectively — one of the reasons perhaps is that we are perceived by society to be rather faceless and impersonal, conservative and reactionary, and not really to be trusted because of our narrow preoccupation with the task of making money.***

Essentially, the aim here is to transfer development capacity from the rich countries to the poor — to stabilize raw material prices — and open up markets in the rich countries for goods produced in the poor countries. I believe that if the chairman and/or chief executive officers of the 100 biggest corporations in the world today came together up in the Norwegian mountains or on a small Pacific island somewhere, they would find a way to reach the unreachable star: A master plan for helping the politicians save the world and all the children who are dying. Nothing more, nothing less!***

Many small brooks make a big river, as we say in Norway, and the opposite of love is not hate but indifference. Life is like a tug-of-war — between ambitions and compassion, facts and feelings, heads and hearts, winners and losers, dreams and so-called realities. I think it was Robert Kennedy who said that "some people see things as they are and ask WHY — I dream of things that never were and ask WHY NOT?"

It hurts the flickering soul. Thank you.

— *Norwegian-American Chamber of Commerce, New York, September 30, 1981*

Thankfully, Knut's vision about the 100 biggest corporations getting together up in the mountains to tackle the world's biggest problems is now happening each year at the World Economic Forum (WEF) in Davos, Switzerland — thanks to the shared vision of Professor Klaus Schwab and the many international corporations and other organizations that support the forum.

Progress is being made, and the more examples we have and models to follow, the sooner creative capitalism will be able, to use Bill Gates' expression, "take wing," or, to use Mackey's expression, "reach the take-off point."

Throughout his career, like most other leaders, Knut has faced challenges that called upon his conscience, his inner compass, to steer a course that he believes to be right but which may or may not be "popular."

Conscience must guide every aspect of one's life and work. In the business arena, the goal must be to achieve commercial success in ways that honor ethical values and respect people, communities and the environment. Although intangible assets, such as leadership, innovation, vision, creativity, willingness to take risks, corporate social responsibility, etc., are not measured, nor often even reported in corporate financial statements, these assets are every bit as important as physical and financial assets in terms of creating value and long-term wealth. In the "owner-entrepreneurial" model of capitalism, the interests of the owner and shareholder are aligned. But in the era of institutionalized ownership, intangible assets — like a corporate conscience and a deeper sense of purpose — can be lost.

Knut's entrepreneurial ventures provide stunning examples of how value is created through intangibles such as vision, courage, conviction, risk-taking, conscience and compassion.

One intangible which is not seen very often in the capital markets today is patience. Yes, patience. In today's world, there is much too much emphasis on short-term performance, rather than long-term value creation. It is a worrisome trend, to be sure. Long-term wealth creation — such as human capital, technology, innovation, supplier alliances, environmental performance, reputation and brand — are often sacrificed on the altar of near-term profit maximization.

All too often institutional and speculative investors are detached from the businesses in which they have invested. They are "owners" but they don't act like owners; they act like speculators. The result is that management is diverted from achieving the company's strategic objectives, competitiveness is weakened, and investments in research and development as well as in environmental performance are sacrificed to meet quarterly earnings expectations. Instead of a partnership of interests organized to create wealth, many corporations are being bought and sold like real estate. John Sunderland, former Chairman of Cadbury Schweppes, was quoted in a *Financial Times* article, *The Short-Term Shareholders Changing the Face of Capitalism (3-28-06)*, as saying:

> I may be old-fashioned but I view a shareholder as a shareholder — someone whose interests in the success and prospects of the company last more than three weeks…I have real concerns about promoting the use of my company's stock as hedge fund plays — just as I would if they were chips in a casino.

Every industry has the opportunity now to reinvent itself in ways that address the world's difficult social, economic and environmental problems. In each case, it will be a matter of conscience — using our businesses to make money, yes, but also steering a course toward a more just and equitable global economy and a healthier Planet Earth. So whether you call it creative capitalism or conscious capitalism or conscientious capitalism or just corporate social responsibility, it all adds up to doing the right thing and for the right reasons. In this, Knut Utstein Kloster has been an exemplar.

"Kind-hearted Capitalist"

CHAPTER NINE
Green Clean Global Village®

Knut's wonderful and exciting vision of a 21st century
hospitality product ("city-at-sea") that can follow peak seasons
and good weather and bring together the best civilization has
to offer in terms of recreation, education, culture and personal
enrichment — while contributing meaningfully to our common
quest for a better future — is nonetheless short of perfect. It is
not a zero-emission vessel.

There are no commercially available technologies that will
permit the vessel to sail without releasing some emissions into
the atmosphere. The city-ship will be powered by GE gas turbines
which have the lowest possible impact on the environment,
including invisible smoke at any power, lower emissions than
traditional marine diesel engines, low particulates, no heavy fuel
sludge byproduct, and utilizing cleaner burning marine gas oil. A
special Selective Catalytic Reduction system (SCR) is installed on
the exhaust of the turbine, suppressing NOX and CO. In addition,
there will be a flue cleaning system of scrubbers incorporated
into the ship's funnels which further cleans the exhaust before it

enters the atmosphere.

The ship will consume the lowest amount of fuel per passenger of any ship in the world. It will utilize solar, wind and wave energy to the maximum extent practical, and it will sail at slow speeds most of the time, which reduces emissions. Since the ship is the destination, long voyages are not contemplated, and coastwise itineraries are planned so that the ship can be accessed by over a 100 million passengers who are within an hour of a point of embarkation, be it by automobile, bus or train. This is a huge fuel savings in terms of air travel normally associated with a cruise vacation.

In addition, the operation of the ship will be making money for World City Foundation and its larger goals, including global environment and development initiatives; and the ship itself will be used as a global forum for important international events and activities. There will be classes, seminars and lectures designed to educate and inform guests and meeting attendees on ways in which they can personally, professionally and organizationally contribute to the search for solutions to our common environmental, societal and economic challenges.

Pending the availability of technologies that will enable the city-ship to operate as a zero-emission vessel, such as small modular atomic engines, the engine and fuel storage capacities of the city-ship have been reconfigured so that when such technologies are approved for commercial use, they can be added without a major conversion. In the interim, Knut and World City America will continue to search for solutions for the creation of a zero-emission ship that can serve as an example and demonstrate that shipping and marine pollution need not be synonymous.

Biosphere at Risk

While many climate experts were, for a time, generally in agreement that global warming is a serious threat to the planet, some climatologists now question the trend and even warn of a new "Little Ice Age."[17] While the dynamics of climate change are complex and subject to differing theories as to cause and effect, civilization cannot ignore the possibility that a buildup of greenhouse gases could, in the century ahead, destabilize the entire biosphere, causing sea levels to rise, creating extreme temperatures, violent storms, devastating droughts, the spread of disease, and the destruction of food production and human habitability in many areas of the globe.

Knut has correctly observed that "The public doesn't know what to believe, but we all understand that oil is a precious resource that our generation should not be squandering, and we all understand that CO_2[18] emissions are polluting our air, damaging our health and that of future generations."

Sailing smokestacks

Global shipping is responsible for a very substantial part of total CO_2 emissions. The United States Congressional Research Service (CRS) reported in 2008 that there were over 46,000 commercial vessels sailing the seven seas, including tankers,

---

[17] *The Economist,* September 27, 2008, citing, e.g., Dr. Philip Stott, Emeritus professor of biogeography, University of London.

[18] CO_2 (carbon dioxide) - a colorless, odorless, non-combustible greenhouse gas that is formed by complete combustion of fossil fuels and carbon-containing products; it also is released through respiration by living organisms and by the gradual oxidation of organic matter in soil. CO_2 is generally believed to contribute to global warming. BusinessDictionary.com

bulk carriers, container ships, barges and passenger ships.

The air pollution is generated by diesel engines that burn high sulfur content fuel, producing sulfur dioxide, nitrogen oxide and particulate matter, in addition to carbon monoxide, carbon dioxide and hydrocarbons. Most commercial ships rely on residual fuel oil, also called "bunker fuel," which is a tar-like sludge left over from the refining of petroleum. Bunker fuel is cheap, less than two-thirds the rate of marine gas oil, according to a report in the *Wall Street Journal*.[19] Cruise ship operators do not use bunker fuel; they use an ultra-low sulfur diesel fuel (ULSD), which has a much lesser impact on the environment. Even so, World City chose to specify GE's gas turbines which use an even cleaner burning marine gas oil. Nonetheless, the impact of commercial shipping on the environment is extremely serious and Knut has decided that he might be able to use his reputation and experience as a shipping executive to advance public awareness of and technical solutions to the marine pollution problem. Except for ports and coastal regions, marine pollution often escapes notice, which is how and why the problem has grown to such seemingly unmanageable proportions.

The above-referenced *Wall Street Journal* report claims that "Ships release more sulfur dioxide, a sooty pollutant associated with acid rain, than all the world's cars, trucks and buses combined," citing a recent study by the International Council on Clean Transportation (ICCT).[20]

The referenced *Wall Street Journal* article continues to cite

---

[19] Ships Draw Fire for Rising Role in Air Pollution, by Bruce Stanley, November 27, 2007.

[20] The International Council on Clean Transportation (ICCT) was formed in 2001 for the purpose of improving the environmental performance of cars, trucks, buses and transportation systems in order to protect and improve public health, the environment and quality of life. www.theicct.org

the ICCT study stating that "ships produced an estimated 27% of the world's smog-causing nitrogen oxide emissions in 2005. Only six countries in the world emitted more greenhouse gases than were produced collectively in 2001 by all ships larger than 100 tons, according to the study and United Nations statistics." (The ICCT study entitled *"Air Pollution and Greenhouse Gas Emissions from Ocean-going Ships"* can be found on ICCT's website: http://www.theicct.org/documents/48_06_ICCT_OceanReportComplete_04-4_taiwanRe).

As Knut observed, even if it is ultimately concluded that CO_2 is not a cause of global warming or that global warming is not being caused by human activity, there are other threats from increased atmospheric concentrations of CO_2. Ocean acidification, which occurs when CO_2 in the atmosphere reacts with water to create carbonic acid, has already increased ocean acidity by 30 percent according to Woods Hole Senior Scientist Scott Doney, who specializes in marine biogeochemistry and ecosystem dynamics and is considered an expert on the global carbon cycle. The full effect of ocean acidification on marine ecosystems and organisms that inhabit them are not yet known, but scientists and policymakers are concerned.

According to Doney, ocean acidification leads to wholesale shifts in seawater carbonate chemistry and will severely impact many organisms that build shells from calcium carbonate (e.g., corals, algae, plankton) by the end of this century. Doney believes that changes in the water cycle and ocean circulation will likely decrease the ability of the land biosphere and oceans to store carbon and that the resulting carbon-climate feedbacks could impact climate change. (*"The Dangers of ocean acidification," Scientific American,* 294 [3], March, 2006, 58-65.)

Although much research remains to be done in this area, the trend of ocean acidification is understandably disconcerting when considering the devastating consequences that acid rain had on freshwater ecosystems during the last century. "Acidification impacts on processes so fundamental to the overall structure and function of marine ecosystems that any significant changes could have far-reaching consequences for the oceans of the future and the millions of people that depend on its food and other resources for their livelihoods," reports Doney.[21] Scientists believe that the combination of warming, rising sea levels, pollution, overfishing and acidification threaten to disrupt the ocean's well-balanced chemical and biological processes. Reducing carbon dioxide emissions will be critical to minimizing these threats. Ocean currents circulate the energy and water that regulate our climate and weather, affecting every part of the human experience.

Oceana, a not-for-profit organization that campaigns to protect and restore the world's oceans, published a comprehensive report which takes the position that the shipping industry is responsible for a significant portion of the climate change problem and of ocean acidification (http://www.oceana.org/shipping-impacts).

The global shipping industry is virtually unregulated, although the International Maritime Organization (IMO), a specialized agency of the United Nations, was created to develop and maintain a comprehensive regulatory framework for shipping, including safety, environmental concerns, technical cooperation and maritime security. The IMO was established to adopt legislation, but individual member governments are

[21] *The Annual Review of Marine Science,* March 2009, 1:169-92

charged with implementing those regulations. The problem, of course, is that some countries lack the experience, expertise and resources necessary to do this properly. Others "put enforcement fairly low down on their list of priorities," the IMO concedes.

The IMO International Convention for the Prevention of Pollution from Ships (MARPOL) affirms the right of a coastal state to take measures to protect its coastline and, in the United States, California and Alaska have passed laws to regulate emissions and other marine pollution. The UK and Baltic States have also enacted legislation to protect their coastal regions.

In 1990, the IMO passed the International Convention on Oil Pollution Preparedness, Response and Cooperation (OPRC), which provides a global framework for international cooperation in regulating and preventing marine pollution, but it operates on a consensus basis. Despite the IMO's good intentions, it is clear that the problems are bigger than the mechanisms in place for dealing with them.

Greenhouse gas emissions from ships are not currently regulated by the United States government or limited under the Kyoto Protocol or other international treaties that address global warming. Pressure is mounting and environmental and other citizen groups are taking action into their own hands. In July of 2008, for example, a coalition of conservation groups and state attorneys general threatened to sue the U.S. Environmental Protection Agency for its failure to address global warming pollution from ocean-going ships. Earthjustice, an environmental law firm that is handling the matter, estimates that a single ship coming into harbor can generate the smog-forming emissions of 350,000 new cars. Earthjustice claims that ship exhaust has been linked to respiratory illness, cancer, heart disease and premature death.

California has passed a law that requires ships within 24 miles of its coastline to burn low sulfur fuel in their auxiliary engines. Los Angeles and Long Beach, the nation's two largest container ports, are encouraging ships to approach ports at slower speeds, which will reduce emissions, and they have provided facilities whereby ships can turn off their engines and receive their power from ashore.

"For a long time," Knut said, "people assumed that the oceans were big enough to cope with any pollution caused by human activity. But we now know this is not the case." The oceans cover over 70 percent of the globe and are the Earth's largest and most important ecosystems. They control our climate and are the primary source of protein for a billion people around the world. "As one of the leading sources of carbon dioxide emissions and other greenhouse gases, the shipping industry has a huge responsibility, as do all other sectors of the global economy, to embrace solutions that will start to reverse the damage," Knut said in a recent interview.

Global shipping activity has increased by three percent per year for the last three decades and this rate of growth is projected to go up. Unless something is done to reduce the use of residual oil (bunker) and other steps taken which will reduce emissions and improve the efficiency of vessels, predications are that shipping pollution will double from 2002 levels by the year 2020 and triple those levels by 2030.

While cruise ships represent a small fraction of the entire shipping industry, they nonetheless can have a serious impact on the environment, depending on how the operator deals with wastes, including sewage, solid waste, graywater, ballast water and oily bilge water. Cruise ship emissions are cleaner than other types of ships, but they still contribute to the pollution of the air and water.

Call to Action — Green Clean Global Village®

As a pioneer in the shipping industry, Knut saw an opportunity to leverage his leadership, experience, and concern for the environment to spearhead a major movement in the maritime industry. The overall goal would be to dramatically reduce marine pollution and, at the same time, work to increase public awareness of the planet's environmental and energy problems and the role each of us can play in the search for solutions. Knowledge and information are great tools in the battle to engage public opinion and participation.

It became clear to Knut that the city-ship project — because of its revolutionary scale and anticipated visibility as one of the world's largest manmade floating structures — has the potential of playing an important role, as exemplar — not just for the burgeoning cruise sector but for the entire shipping industry. The goal is to ultimately create a zero-emission, wholly energy-efficient, totally environmentally benign vessel. Such a ship could serve as an energy demonstration platform and an energy research center where new wind, solar and wave technologies are efficiently utilized as supplements to a main 100 MW(e) atomic engine which simultaneously produces hydrogen for the ship's fuel cells. "It's a simple concept, but difficult to implement," Knut said, "and for all the wrong reasons. There are a lot of misconceptions about nuclear energy in commercial applications. But," he added, "there is no way around it for the future of the planet. What I envision is a self-sustaining ship, or village, producing its own water, responsibly treating its own waste, and not generating any pollution — a Clean Green Global Village®."

Knut's sea-going version of a Green Clean Global Village (GCGV) would also fill the city-ship's original mission by making money as a destination resort while serving as a global forum — welcoming thought-leaders, scientists, business executives, government officials, professors, teachers and concerned citizens. Our children and grandchildren would see that it is possible to enjoy 21st century amenities and pleasures without taxing the environment or future generations.

Terrestrial energy is the solution — it's sustainable, safe and green

In his 2008 book, *Terrestrial Energy: How Nuclear Power Will Lead the Green Revolution and End America's Energy Odyssey*, veteran journalist William Tucker explains that nuclear energy is "terrestrial" — the same process that heats the center of the earth. Tucker points out that "every fuel used in human history... has been derived from the sun. But," he explained in a *Wall Street Journal* article (July 21, 2008), "terrestrial energy is different":

> Terrestrial energy is the heat at the earth's core that raises its temperature to 7,000 degrees Fahrenheit, hotter than the surface of the sun. Remarkably, this heat derives largely from a single source — the radioactive breakdown of uranium and thorium. The energy released in the breakdown of these two elements is enough to melt iron,

stoke volcanoes and float the earth's continents like giant
barges on its molten core.

Geothermal plants are a way of tapping this heat. They
are generally located near fumaroles and geysers, where
groundwater meets hot spots in the earth's crust. If we
dig down far enough, however, we will encounter more
than enough heat to boil water. Engineers are now
talking about drilling down 10 miles (the deepest oil wells
are only five miles) to tap this energy.

Here's a better idea: Bring the source of this heat — the
uranium — to the surface, put it in a carefully controlled
environment, and accelerate its breakdown a bit to raise
temperatures to around 700 degrees Fahrenheit, and use
it to boil water. That's what we do in a nuclear reactor.

Tucker's use of the word "terrestrial" ("from the land" or "from
the earth") accurately describes nuclear *energy* and helps remove
the stigma associated with nuclear *weaponry.*

A year-long investigation into the pros and cons of
"terrestrial" energy as playing an important role in addressing
marine pollution over time and providing a viable path to a zero-
emission Green Clean Global Village® at sea led Knut and World
City America Inc. to conclude that nuclear energy can eventually
provide a clean, safe, reliable and competitive energy source for
the industry. There are a number of new advanced, small, next-
generation atomic plants being developed for use in remote
villages across the globe that do not have access to electricity,
and several of these technologies are compatible with use at sea.

Knut shares the view that nuclear power must be part of the
energy mix if we are to replace a significant part of the fossil fuels
(coal, oil and gas) which massively pollute the atmosphere and

are believed to contribute to the greenhouse gas effect.

The disaster in Japan after the earthquake and tsunami taught some important lessons, but it did not change the reality that nuclear power is the only green energy source that can meet rising energy needs, particularly in the emerging economies. But there must be more focus on safety and common sense in the placement of reactors. The situation in Japan was an accident waiting to happen and, with proper planning, much of damage to the Fukushima Daiichi Nuclear Power Station could have been avoided. The reactors at Fukushima date from the 1960s, but there are still precautions that could have been taken, given its location. The new next-generation reactors offer a much safer, reliable, and proliferation proof solution, but placement of the reactors will always be an issue and may require additional fortification in areas subject to natural disasters such as earthquakes and floods.

The United States has over 100 nuclear reactors providing approximately 20% of the nation's energy. After twenty years of steady decline in the industry, several factors have fueled a resurgence, but experts predict the process will be slowed as a result of the Fukushima disaster. The United States government is standing behind its commitment to significant R&D funding with the objective of rebuilding the nation's leadership in nuclear technologies. Over the past two decades, the industry has been working with the Nuclear Regulatory Commission (NRC) to certify a number of third generation advanced reactor designs. Several of these new designs were found by the NRC to dramatically exceed safety goals. The Energy Policy Act of 2005 provides many incentives for the nuclear power industry including tax credits, risk insurance, loan guarantees and additional support for advanced nuclear technologies. None of this has changed after Fukushima.

Research and Development on nuclear energy in the United States has taken place at a number of Department of Energy laboratories, particularly the Idaho National Engineering and Environmental Laboratory (INEEL, formerly INL), as well as at numerous universities. Focus is on advanced, next-generation nuclear power systems for both electricity and hydrogen production. The goal is to develop a plant that will be smaller, safer, more flexible, and more cost-effective than any commercial nuclear plant in history and clear the way for the long-term future of the industry, as well as a way to replace imported oil with domestically produced, clean and economic hydrogen.

In February 2006, the U.S. government announced a Global Nuclear Energy Partnership (GNEP) whereby it "will work with other nations possessing advanced nuclear technologies to develop new proliferation-resistant technologies in order to produce more energy, reduce waste and minimize proliferation concerns." As part of this initiative, partner nations will develop a program whereby nuclear fuel is provided to developing nations which will allow them to enjoy the benefits of nuclear energy in exchange for agreeing to forego enrichment and reprocessing activities. This program will further alleviate proliferation concerns.

The World City technical team, led by Tage Wandborg, World City's naval architect, and Dick Baumler, its marine engineer, researched various near-term atomic energy technologies which might be suitable for marine application.

Terrestrial energy is a necessary component in addressing the energy crisis

Despite the continued existence of a highly vocal anti-nuclear movement — all the more so after the Fukushima disaster — Knut and the World City team have been persuaded that atomic energy remains one of the best solutions to environmental public health problems, as well as a necessary and probably central part of any effort to meet the world's increasing energy demands. "The benefits of nuclear energy are real," says Larry Foulke, past president of the American Nuclear Society and co-author of Dispelling the Myths About Nuclear Power, a brief prepared for the National Center for Policy Analysis:

> When decisions are made concerning future sources of
> electric power in the United States, facts, not fear, should
> be the basis for appraising the nuclear industry's place in
> the mix.

James Lovelock, creator of the Gaia Theory that Earth is a single self-regulating organism (see Chapter Six), was anti-nuclear for many years but has since concluded that nuclear power is the last, best hope for averting what he calls "climatic catastrophe." It was Lovelock who encouraged Knut and World City to look into the possibility of atomic energy for the city-ship. According to Lovelock:

> The worldwide use [of nuclear power] as our main source
> of energy would pose an insignificant threat compared
> with the dangers of intolerable and lethal heat waves and
> sea levels rising to drown every coastal city of the world.
> We have no time to experiment with visionary energy

sources; civilization is in imminent danger and has to
use nuclear, the one safe, available energy source, now,
or suffer the pain soon to be inflicted by our outraged
planet.

Patrick Moore, one of the founders of Greenpeace and its
Director for many years, has joined Lovelock and many other
environmental activists in converting from anti-nuclear to
pro-nuclear on the basis of solid scientific facts, as well as
environmental realities.

After the Fukushima Daiichi accident, I contacted Jim
Lovelock and several other nuclear energy advocates mentioned
in this book to see if their positions had changed or modified
as a result of this incident. Here, in part, is what Jim Lovelock had
to say:

It is true that the slowly improving perception of nuclear
energy was dashed by the reaction of the world media to
the Fukushima event…but I stand by what I have said in
the past. We need safe, secure and inexpensive nuclear
energy to sustain the supply of electricity to our cities.
There is no carbon-free alternative.

Jim also told me that he found it "obscene" the way the media
has used the nuclear accident to sell newspapers and space on
television while ignoring the intense suffering of the Japanese
people. "Where else in the world," he asked, "would any kind of
industrial installation withstand a Richter 9 earthquake followed
by a 10 metre tsunami? In fact, the plant at Fukushima withstood
both of these blows but failed only because of the failure of its
cooling water supply."

The nuclear energy advocates with whom I have spoken

or whose opinions I have researched for this Second Edition understand that safety issues have already been addressed by the Generation III and IV reactor designs. They maintain that the lessons learned from the Fukushima accident will guide the industry in the future in terms of the placement of reactors and precautions that were unfortunately not taken by Japanese nuclear regulatory authorities. For a well-rounded discussion on the subject, visit the Milken Institute's website [milkeninstitute. org] and a session at the 2011 Global Conference entitled "Nuclear Energy After Fukushima" [http://www.milkeninstitute. org/events/gcprogram.taf?function=detail&EvID=2530&eventid =GC11].

Gwyneth Cravens has also written an important book, *Power to Save the World: The Truth About Nuclear Energy*, in which she dispels decades of misinformation and misconceptions about nuclear energy. Cravens' comprehensive and compelling narrative debunks every argument that has been advanced by the anti-nuclear movement and forces the conclusion that nuclear energy is the only real solution to the world's increasing energy demands and the hazards associated with burning fossil fuels. Another valuable work on the subject is *The GeoPolitics of Energy: Achieving a Just and Sustainable Energy Distribution by 2040* by Judith Wright and James Conca.

More than ever before, corporate leaders and individuals are stepping up and taking a stand on important issues such as the climate and energy crises. Knut saw the advantages of tapping into that encouraging movement and leveraging the potential benefits of his own public awareness campaign and the Green Clean Global Village® initiative.

Sergey Brin and Larry Page, Google's founders, have

committed billions of dollars to helping to solve the world's "biggest, most imminent, and least well-resourced problems," including global poverty, global health and sustainable development. As part of this ambitious agenda, Google is committed to helping build a "clean and green energy future."

Google plans to use its enormous IT clout to advocate public policy that will "accelerate the development and deployment of cost-effective, energy-efficient, and renewable energy technologies in order to achieve deep and rapid reductions in greenhouse gas emissions".

On the energy front, google.org launched a multi-billion dollar strategic initiative whose mission is to develop electricity from renewable sources cheaper than electricity produced from coal (RE<C) and to do it in years, not decades. The announced focus is on solar thermal power, wind power technologies and enhanced geothermal systems.

Jesse H. Ausubel, Director, Program for the Human Environment at The Rockefeller University (http://phe.rockefeller.edu/jesse/) was one of the main organizers of the first UN World Climate Conference in Geneva in 1979. He was also the main author of the 1983 report, *Changing Climate*, which was the first comprehensive analysis of the greenhouse effect. Ausubel considers himself a "heretic" among Greens. He argues that renewable sources of energy, such as solar and wind, are not green. "To reach a scale at which they would contribute importantly to meeting global energy demand, renewable sources of energy, such as wind, water and biomass, cause serious environmental harm."

> "Cheerful self-delusion about new solar and renewables since 1970," says Ausubel, "has yet to produce a single

quad of the more than 90 quadrillion BTU of total energy
the U.S. now yearly consumes...Let's stop sanctifying
false and minor gods..."

— *Renewable and Nuclear Heresies, Int. J. Nuclear
Governance, Economy and Ecology, Vol. 1, No. 3, 2007.*

According to Ausubel, technologies succeed when economics
of scale are present — when the technologies grow smaller even
as they become more powerful, like computer chips. In other
words, if an energy system is to grow, it must shrink in size and
cost. "Considered in watts per square metre," argues Ausubel,
"nuclear has astronomical advantages over its competitors."
However, if the nuclear industry is to meet its full potential, it
must expand out of its niche market, i.e., providing baseload
electricity, and start making hydrogen as well. Ausubel sees
methane as the means for accomplishing this. (See "*The Future
Market for the Energy Business," APPEA Journal* 2007, Part 2, pp.
487-494)

Knut says it would be interesting to put Ausubel in the same
room with Messrs. Page and Brin, as well as other energy experts,
to explore the perceived (or misperceived) advantages of solar
and wind technologies which Ausubel insists simply are not
green and will never generate a fraction of the planet's baseload
electricity requirements:

> They may be renewable but calculating spatial density
> proves they are not green. The best way to understand
> the scale of destruction that hydro, biomass, wind and
> solar promise is to denominate each in watts/m2 that the
> source could produce. In a well-watered area like Ontario,
> Canada, 1 km2 produces enough hydroelectricity for
> about a dozen Canadians while severely damaging life

in its rivers. A biomass power plant requires about 2,400 km2 of prime Iowa farmland to equal the output of a single 1,000 MW nuclear power plant on a few hectares. Windmills to equal the same nuclear plant cover about 800 km2 in a very favorable climate. Photovoltaics require less but still need a carpet of 150 km2 to match the nuclear plant.***

No economics of scale adhere to any of the solar and renewable sources, so trying to supply India or eastern China would require increases in infrastructure that would overwhelm these already crowded lands. Moreover, the photovoltaics raise nasty problems of hazardous materials. Wind farms irritate with low frequency noise and thumps, blight landscapes, and whack birds and bats. And solar and renewables in every form require large and complex machinery to produce many megawatts. While a natural gas combined cycle plant uses 3.3 metric tons (mt) of steel and 27 m3 of concrete, a typical wind energy system requires construction inputs of 460 mt of steel and 870 m3 of concrete per average MW(e), about 130 and 30 times as much. Bridging the cloudy and dark as well as calm and gusty weather take storage batteries and their heavy metals. Burning crops inflates the price of food. Renewable energies also invoke high risks as sources of supply in a changing climate. Clouds may cover the deserts investors covered with photovoltaics. Rain may no longer fall where we built dams and planted biomass for fuel. The wind may no longer blow where we build windmills.***

Without vastly improved storage, the windmills and photovoltaics are supernumeraries for the coal, methane and uranium plants that operate reliably around the clock day after day. We live in an era of mass delusions about solar and other renewables, which will become an embarrassing collection of stranded assets. But let's use

our intelligence and resources to build what will work on
the large scale that matters for decarbonization rather
than to fight irrationality.

*— Renewable and Nuclear Heresies, Int. J. Nuclear
Governance, Economy and Ecology,* Vol. 1, No. 3, pp. 229-
243, 2007.

World City's research, including reading the work of and often
making contact with some of the nation's and world's most
prominent organizations, scientists and environmentalists, as
well as authors, government officials and corporate and business
leaders in the energy field, led Knut to conclude that nuclear
energy provides the only green solution to baseload (large scale)
energy requirements, both here at home and in developing
nations. Renewables such as wind, solar and geothermal, while
worth pursuing for niche applications, could not begin to
deliver energy on a scale that is required now, let alone in the
decades to come and in places such as China and India where
energy requirements are escalating at a phenomenal pace. There
appears to be very little legitimate basis for disagreement with
this proposition.

Nor can wind and solar even begin to provide the power
requirements of World City's city-ship or the globe's expanding
merchant fleet if it is to back away from residual oil and other
fossil fuels that have such a devastating impact on the health of
the environment and our oceans' complex ecosystem.

Knut's goal is simply to gather the best and the brightest
brains on the energy issue and to meet with world business
leaders, including Google's leadership, in the hope of enlisting
their participation in the campaign to promote a science-based
debate on nuclear energy, as well as to seek encouragement of

the campaign to reform the shipping industry. Knut genuinely believes that his Green Clean Global Village® initiative is poised to play an important role in that challenge.

CHAPTER TEN
Little United Nations at Sea (LUNAS)

"And he shall judge among the nations, and shall rebuke many people: and they shall beat their swords into plowshares, and their spears into pruning hooks: nation shall not lift up sword against nation, neither shall they learn war any more."
— Isaiah 2:4

For more than two decades, Knut has been captivated by the concept of a Little United Nations at Sea (LUNAS) — a ship that would travel the world, represent all nations, and have as her mission simply bringing people together to search for solutions to humankind's biggest problems. He sees LUNAS as a messenger of peace and a mediator of disputes between countries and cultures. He envisions that the ship will fly the UN flag, with the flags of all nations of the world also represented.

Knut asked Tage Wandborg to design such a ship and the result is *GAIASHIP.*

The LUNAS concept and *GAIASHIP* were endorsed by the late eminent scientist, writer, and futurist, Sir Arthur C. Clarke, who wrote in a letter to Knut:

> I think it is an excellent idea — a proposal of global
> significance — the kind of collaborative international
> venture that our world needs now more than ever.***

Illustration of GAIASHIP globe by Terje Olsen

There is nothing like a ship voyage to create a feeling of unity, as well as a better understanding of the wonderful planet on which we live. This would be an investment for a more peaceful future for all of us.

The proposed *GAIASHIP* is 767 feet long, carrying 1,072 passengers and an international crew of 520. The Gaia Globe, in the center of the ship — reminiscent of Planet Earth as seen from outer space — is the ship's signature attribute. The Gaia Globe would serve as a joint reminder of our global interdependence and the frailty of our Planet Earth. The World Future Society (WFS) also endorsed the concept and the ship was featured in The Futurist,[22] a magazine published by the Society. In a letter of support from Edward Cornish, President of the Society, he writes:

> The World Future Society (WFS) strongly and unreservedly endorses the aims of the GAIASHIP as presented to us and fully supports the proposed joint activity between the WFS and the Sir Arthur C. Clarke Foundation on board the vessel.
>
> At present, over 90 percent of WFS activities take place within the United States. However, the Society has now declared its intention to become much more international in its operations: to become a World Future Society in effect as well as in name.
>
> We believe that *GAIASHIP* could be the ideal vehicle to carry the WFS message to the rest of the world. We also see the vessel as a highly suitable base for our annual conferences, seminars and other events.

[22] *The Futurist* – Vol. 36, No. 6

> The World Future Society sees every benefit from the
> realization of the *GAIASHIP* project and is happy to join
> Sir Arthur in recommending it to all.

A future studies center is also planned in collaboration with the World Future Society and The Arthur C. Clarke Foundation. The center will be named in honor of Sir Arthur C. Clarke.

As mentioned in Chapter Three, Knut had arranged with the United Nations to have the UN Flag flown on board the *S/S NORWAY*. That may have been the seed that grew into the LUNAS concept. In 1985, Knut made a statement about how *M/S LITTLE UNITED NATIONS* could help make the world a better place. Here are some excerpts:

> A World Center at sea. Not land-based or located in
> any one country, but sailing under the UN flag from
> continent to continent...Linking the world together by
> moving around as a focus for the expression of global
> perspectives...Result-oriented in terms of solutions to
> problems and identifying opportunities for development
> in the fields of culture, economy, education,
> environment, health, research, etc.***

> The ports of call to be chosen as appropriate sites
> for conclaves which by nature and content of each
> occasion, and the presence of those attending, support
> the objectives. On the crossings between ports the ship
> would carry regular passengers as well as the participants
> in planned events, such as conferences, conventions
> and seminars. Also perhaps a symbolic mini-community
> composed of ordinary families from different parts of
> the world potentially impacted by the subjects to be
> discussed and debated.

The ship will be the base for a secretariat that will
organize the process, link the conclaves together
and ensure that the world's focus on the project is
maintained. A group of renowned universities will
be invited to participate. A highly sophisticated
mass media center onboard will provide for direct,
continuous satellite communication between the ship
and all corners of the world. Maybe sponsorship could
be established jointly by the three biggest and most
influential countries in the world — USSR, USA and
China? Alternatively, the project could be financed
through a combination of private enterprise, special
allocations, fees and grants, sale of TV and publishing
rights, etc. Significant revenue could undoubtedly also
be generated by all the activities without jeopardizing
the project's integrity.

Knut genuinely believes that the LUNAS concept has merit
and, over the years, has explored ways to promote the idea.
For example, in 2009, Knut published a small flyer about LUNAS
("An idea whose time has come") and had over 10,000 copies
of it distributed by student volunteers at the United Nations
Climate Change Conference held in Copenhagen.

Picking up on the Isaiah quote under the chapter heading
above, he wrote:

The idea is to promote peace and international
cooperation by converting a tiny fraction of UN member
nations' military spending into a Little United Nations
at Sea — a global communications center that will sail
around the world on the seven seas, flying the UN flag
and the flags of all nations, reaching out and touching
people where they live on five continents, respecting
all cultures, all beliefs, and the aspirations of the world's
children.

To make the idea a reality, Knut suggested that the UN Security Council agree to divert a tiny fraction of their military spending to a UN fund set up to build and operate LUNAS. He proposed that contributions could also be made by individuals, corporations and organizations dedicated to international peace, sustainable development and global security.

Kloster, a shipping man with five decades of experience, estimated that the cost of building LUNAS would be about the same as building a small frigate. "Frigate into peace ship = spears into pruning hooks," he said, "transcending all religions and in defense of transnational threats such as environmental degradation, global poverty, and energy shortages."

Knut has also suggested LUNAS could be financed, built and operated by oil-rich Norway. "Not that long ago," he says, "Norway was one of the poorest countries in Europe. Today it is one of the richest, thanks to oil. Our national fortune per capita is immense. In a global perspective, sponsoring the creation of LUNAS by Norway, for the benefit of the United Nations and world peace, would be a good investment, pure and simple."

Knut firmly believes that tomorrow's hidden enemy, and the major threat to national and international security, is the environment. He quotes a report published by WORLD WATCH (May/June 1999) written by two leading authorities on U.S. national security, Gregory D. Foster, Professor of National Security Studies at the Industrial College of the Armed Forces, National Defense University where he previously has served as George C. Marshall Professor, J. Carlton Ward Distinguished Professor and Director of Research, and executive director of the Defense Environmental Forum, a joint activity of the Deputy Under Secretary of Defense, and the president of the National

Defense University; together with Louise B. Wise, President
of Wise Solutions LLC, a senior fellow at Harvard's Kennedy
School of Government, a member of the Council on Foreign
Relations, and the founder and first Secretariat Director of the
Global Development Alliance (U.S. Agency for International
Development [USAID]) which forges strategic alliances
between public and private partners in addressing international
development issues:

> The environment is the most transnational of all
> transnational issues. In both its origins and its reach,
> it respects neither national borders nor traditional
> concepts of sovereignty and territorial integrity. To
> acknowledge that the environment constitutes the
> entirety of our surroundings — air, water, land, natural
> resources, wildlife — is to confront two questions of
> fundamental strategic import: first, whether humanity's
> role on Earth is to be nature's master, servant, or steward;
> and second, whether nature's commons, affecting us all,
> demand sustained collective international attention and
> tending...What the concept of sustainable development
> has been to the environmental community, a new notion
> of sustainable security might now be to the U.S. and
> international security community...new ways of thinking
> about and using the military must be at the forefront
> of any security reorientation...we must restructure
> ourselves to reflect new post-Cold War realities and
> challenges.***
>
> — *Transnational Environmental Threats: Tomorrow's
> Hidden Enemy (as printed in WORLD WATCH, May/June
> 1999)*

Knut urges that this new notion of sustainable security
effectively justifies his proposal to divert a tiny fraction of some

military spending to a UN fund set up to build and operate LUNAS. "Frigate into peace ship and plow shares; it makes eminent good sense," he argues, rather persuasively!

As this Second Edition is heading to press, there has been heated debate in Norway over that country's plans to buy a new fleet of fighter jets (F35s) from U.S. contractor, Lockheed Martin, for a cost approaching US$10 billion. While the debate has centered on uncertainty regarding the actual final cost of Norway's participation in this program, and Lockheed's ability to produce and deliver the first jets on the anticipated schedule, Knut looks beyond those concerns to what he sees as the need to invest the same amount of time and energy in peace initiatives, like his idea for a Little United Nations At Sea.

"I can't help but wonder," Knut says, "why Norway wouldn't consider a few fewer F35s and apply the savings to creation of a Little United Nations at Sea.

"If each of the countries involved in the F35 program, e.g., the United States, Italy, Denmark, Turkey, etc., did the same thing," he continues, "imagine the ripple effect…imagine the benefit to national and international security."

In the end, in terms of this story, the point is not whether the UN Security Council or the governments of the United States and Norway can be persuaded to support the LUNAS initiative, but rather, what we all can do, following the excellent example of Knut Utstein Kloster, to stay focused on the possible, to seize every opportunity for peace and good, and to follow our own True North.

"I can't say it better than the Prophet Isaiah," Knut concludes, "and I know that what Isaiah is telling us has been said by the prophets of all religions and faiths, in so many words. We must take it to heart.

"In our times," Knut reminds us, "war is not the only threat. The global environment, resource management, and energy supply are among the transnational issues that must be urgently addressed if international security is to be protected. Enter LUNAS."

Knut's Little United Nations at Sea concept is a 21st century approach to world peace and international understanding — a proposal to convert at least *some* weapons of death and destruction into peaceful tools that are beneficial to the society of nations and to the notion of sustainability. It's a great concept whose time has come.

CHAPTER ELEVEN
DRAGON WORLD CITY — PHOENIX Could Rise in China

Simultaneously with the development of the American Flagship project, Knut and his team have kept a watchful eye on Asia and, particularly, on China. Knut recognized that China was becoming one of the world's major economic powers with the greatest ongoing growth potential. Today, China is the world's second largest economy after the United States. It is generally viewed that China will become the world's largest economy (by nominal GPD) within the decade.

China has, by design, been transitioning itself from an export-dependent economy to a domestic-consumption economy. While wages have been steadily and rapidly rising throughout the country, there has been an enormous and steady migration to China's cities by hundreds of millions of its citizens seeking higher paying jobs. This has resulted in a dramatic emergence of an urban-affluent middle class with significant disposable income. And since this segment is currently concentrated in the biggest cities, it makes it easier to reach and serve them.

Long since recognizing that urban households in China will make up one of the largest consumer markets in the world, Knut and his partners have targeted China as an ideal base for the city-ship concept. A good deal of work has been done to introduce *DRAGON WORLD CITY* to the Chinese government, shipyards, and potential joint venture partners in the leisure/travel/entertainment business.

While Chinese shipyards may not have yet acquired the ability to undertake the type of high value-added ship construction necessary to build passenger ships, they can build the hull and bring in a hotel construction partner, as planned for the construction of the American Flagship. They can also take a stake in a foreign shipyard, as the Koreans have done, to position themselves to acquire the knowledge and experience in passenger ship construction over time.

China's prosperity and its fast-growing middle class have cultivated more sophisticated tastes and habits. China tourism, particularly domestic tourism, has become a key industry for economic development. China's domestic tourism contributes more than 70% of the total tourism revenue. The domestic tourism market in China is expected to grow at an annual rate of 8% over the next decade. The World Trade Organization has forecast that China's tourism industry will capture up to 8.6% of world market share to become the world's top tourism industry by 2020.

DRAGON WORLD CITY, like *AMERICA WORLD CITY*, will be 265,000 GRT but it will be configured to accommodate more guests, including day visitors and overnight guests, and the gaming and retail operations will be considerably more dominant, consistent with consumer trends and interests. The marina and day cruiser concept will be an integral part of the product offering to enable guests to easily check in and check out as the ship moves along the coast. The World City team has done a great deal of work on the *DRAGON WORLD CITY* concept, including developing possible itineraries, making initial contacts with shipyards, and transplanting the virtual shipyard combination of U.S. 5-star hotel construction expertise and project management with commercial shipbuilding as it exists today in China. One of World City's principal team members, Wimberly, Allison, Tong & Goo (WAT&G) has been a lead designer in a wide area of hotel projects in China, including the Ritz-Carlton/Marriott in Beijing and the Sandalwood Private Resorts in Shanghai.

Dr. Joseph West, who serves on World City America Inc.'s Advisory Board, has been working with the Chinese government since 2001 and is well-connected there. As Professor and former Dean of the School of Hospitality and Tourism Management, Florida International University [FIU], Dr. West established a campus in Tianjin, China. Over a thousand Chinese students (and twelve Americans) are enrolled in the FIU program in Tianjin. The government of Tianjin built a $50 million campus to house the FIU program which now nets over $1 million a year — a great help to the Miami campus as the Florida legislature continues to withdraw tax-generated support from state universities.

Dr. West has long supported World City's Young Professional Program® which will draw graduate and undergraduate students from hospitality management schools across the United States to serve internships on board *AMERICA WORLD CITY*. This same type of program is contemplated for *DRAGON WORLD*

CITY, and FIU is ideally positioned to collaborate on the training and staffing for the ship.

While it has not yet been determined which port will serve as home port for *DRAGON WORLD CITY,* the Qingdao Port can accommodate the city-ship and is located in a very beautiful part of the city. The Qingdao Port is used only for passenger ships, whereas the Tianjin Port and the Dalian Port are also used for other commercial maritime activity and are, therefore, not as attractive.

World City's development work in Asia and China was initially handled by World City Asia, Ltd., a Marshall Islands company. However, China's foreign investment climate has changed dramatically with more than two decades of reform, and World City is now planning to form a joint venture with a Chinese company, mostly likely one that is operating in the leisure travel or gaming sector.

Knut enjoys recounting that, in Chinese mythology, Phoenix and Dragon signify wedding bliss. "Phoenix will rise in China as *DRAGON WORLD CITY,*" he said. "It's something we have planned for many years, and I think the time may now have come. It is a very exciting initiative and holds great promise for China's fast-growing tourism industry." Knut is well aware, of course, of China's expanding shipbuilding aspirations. Although China is the world's largest shipbuilder in terms of capacity and new orders, its value-added shipbuilding ability is still behind South Korea and Japan [http://www.marinelink.com/news/shipbuilding-china-step338433.aspxy]. "World City's virtual shipyard approach," Knut claims, "can play a role in helping China bridge that innovation gap, just as it is doing in America."

CHAPTER TWELVE
Friend of Man

"He was a friend to man, and he lived in a house by the side of the road."

— Homer

Not that long ago, it became universally incorrect to speak or write generically about man, men, mankind, as if women didn't exist. Knut took it to the extreme for a while by never failing, no matter how awkward the sentence, paragraph or speech would become, to add "/she" beside the word "he" or "/women" beside the word "men" or to change "mankind" to "humankind" in his writings and communications. That was in the 80s.

True, he comes from one of the few countries that was ahead of its time in terms of recognizing the merits of women in industry and government. So it all probably came easier to him than to most of us in terms of daily use.

With advance apologies, then, for the use of the word "Man"

in this chapter heading, it is taken from the Sam Walter Foss (1858-1911) poem "The House by the Side of the Road." The Homer quote above is also applicable to Knut's unassuming home by the side of the road in the outskirts of Oslo. Knowing that he comes from a venerable Norwegian shipping family, whose prominence in the industry goes back two generations, one would expect something more grand. Knut's house is warm, comfortable and inviting but not large or extravagant in any respect. It fits neatly into the landscape and the neighborhood, right by the side of the road. Foss' poem captures how Knut sees himself and his place in the world:

> "Let me live in a house by the side of the road,
>   Where the race of men go by —
> The men who are good and the men who are bad,
>   As good and as bad as I.
> I would not sit in the scorner's seat,
>   Or hurl the cynic's ban —
> Let me live by the side of the road
>   And be a friend to man."

Knut truly is a friend of man in the universal (man/woman, haves/have nots) context. He has a heart of gold, and it shines through every step he takes and every decision he makes.

Exitus acta probat — By their deeds ye shall know them

Knut's "best" friend over the years has been his German Shepherd. In recent years, there has been Kahnin, Egon and Kelly. In 2010, Knut acquired a Welsh Corgi puppy and named him Gaio.

Knut seen here with Kahnin as a puppy.

Knut's love of animals and respect for nature has been the theme of his entire life. For example, he stood up against whaling in Norway where whaling is deeply rooted in the country's culture, economy and history and where many fellow Norwegians — and the Norwegian government — support whaling, believing that it can be done in a responsible and sustainable manner. For Knut, it was a brutality issue:

> The whale is warm-blooded and feels pain just like human beings. Slowly dying after being harpooned is torture, pure and simple. Biologists say that whales have a nervous system similar to our own and that the animal therefore experiences pain and fear much the same way as we do. The harvesting method is gruesome. Obviously, there are many other animals that also suffer, but we

are now on the subject of whales. There is a relationship
between how we treat animals and how we treat each
other as human beings.

Standing up for employees' rights is another example. As a
shipping executive, Knut always considered it a matter of
conscience, as well as good business, that the crews onboard
his ships were treated with respect and dignity, that they
received fair wages and that they be provided with decent
accommodations and adequate facilities. "The ships are
the *home away from home* for the crew," he said. "This is an
ideological, and also a pragmatic, issue because without a happy
crew, you cannot expect good service or proper maintenance of
the vessels." When Knut was at the helm of NCL, the Caribbean
crews were covered by a general agreement with the Norwegian
Seaman's union. No other cruise operator at that time, or for
many years thereafter, had the same reputation for the crews'
welfare. There is no question that Knut's good example gradually
had an impact on the industry. Today, most of the major cruise
companies have overhauled their policies and now provide
decent minimal accommodations for their crews on the newer,
larger ships.

In the early 70s, Knut was a regular contributor to the
prominent Norwegian business magazine, *KAPITAL*. As in all
aspects of his life, he was never hesitant to speak up for what is
right or to write about subjects that go beyond straight business
and make a broader point or lesson or just show the human
side of life. One article was entitled Åpent hus, or "Open House."
The article started with an anecdote:

One evening some years ago a lot of demonstrators

gathered outside an American Embassy. As usual,
windows were smashed. Suddenly, the lights went on,
the door was opened, and out came the Ambassador
himself. He invited the demonstrators to come in. Coffee
was served and politics was discussed. The lights were
not turned off again until late into the night. Since then,
there has been little, if any, demonstration outside the
Embassy.

At about that time, Knut explained, Finn Gustavsen, the late
Norwegian socialist-politician had appeared on television and
fired what Knut viewed as a very unfair and untruthful salvo
at Norwegian shipowners. The shipping industry in Norway
typically "laid low" and didn't comment on the Gustavsen attack.
Knut felt that the better approach would be to come out, turn on
the lights, and invite the critic to openly debate the issues raised.
This is what the "Open House" article was about. "I don't exactly
believe that Finn Gustavsen would have eaten humble-pie,
but maybe he would be a bit more careful when, the next time
around (in spite of his knowledge), he expressed such opinions,"
Knut wrote.

In some of the articles, Knut talked about love, marriage and
family. In this 1973 piece, he addressed the role of the husband/
father:

> It is Saturday morning, quiet in the office and bad
> weather. In the paper I noted that Bishop Alex Johnson
> and Member of Parliament, Berit Ås, will talk about
> marriage and the family in the old celebration hall at the
> University starting at 10:15. Why not? So, a half an hour
> later I was sitting there, together with lots of women and
> a few men.

"The foundation of marriage is love, and its purpose is happiness," a wise man said in 1799. And thus came into being the myth about marriage as a happiness automaton.*** No, marriage certainly is no happiness automaton, Alex Johnson said. It is a heavy load being pulled by two people together.*** Alex Johnson called the relationship between mother, father and child the "biological triangle," and he did not hide his optimism about the family institution despite all the gloomy predictions about its breaking up and destruction. Marriage and family have a strong position in society, he said, and in his opinion they would prevail in the future.***

Enter Berit Ås. She focused on the women's position in marriage and the family: To what extent today do married women with children experience the so-called "biological triangle" as a living social reality? She referred to findings showing that the father is together with his children only an average of 8 minutes every day (half an hour on Saturdays and Sundays). And then she noted all the other things that make a mother's position so difficult, and her self-image so frail.

In reality, Berit Ås said, strong indications are that the family is one of the weakest institutions we have in society. It's only the man who is clinging to the myth about the family because he needs it as a resource. He is dependent upon having a woman behind him, who takes care of the unsalaried production which housework is. Talking about self-confidence and self-realization are empty phrases in the man's mouth, as long as he is not willing to do something concrete and constructive about it, in his own family and out in society.

Conclusion: Only if the woman is liberated can the family survive. The man in the family has to become just as much of a resource for the woman as the woman is for the man.

Now then, if we take up this gauntlet which Berit Ås and many others have thrown down — and in my opinion we should do that — then we in industry should ask ourselves the following question: Looking ahead, how can we create such conditions that the fathers not only get the opportunity to, but actually become motivated to be at home as "househusbands" a substantial part of their time, while the holes thereby being created in the outside work force are filled by qualified women? How can we realistically start such a process?

Norway has, of course, made great strides in that direction in the intervening decades.

In another article entitled "Cultural Revolution," Knut asked what it would take for privileged society to "reduce our wasteful extravagant consumption" and "get in contact with other qualities of life more valuable than the materialistic." The article focused on the responsibility of rich countries to deal with the realities of the developing world — hunger, suffering, poverty, sickness and overpopulation. He quoted Maurice Strong: "The root of all ills sits in the materialistic- and competition-driven attitudes dominating our whole culture." We must get a social system, Strong is quoted as saying, that places "the economy" in its rightful place, "at the service of social goals." Such statements, Knut writes, are not easily pushed under the carpet, pretending that they have not been heard. Maybe we *do* need a cultural revolution, he suggests.

Being a down-to-earth "friend of man" and a contributing member of his community are every bit as important in Knut's life as his international business ventures spanning many decades and several continents. "Think globally but act locally" is a concept, attributed to René Dubos (acting as an advisor to the United Nations Conference on the Human Environment in 1972), which suggests that global problems can turn into action only by considering ecological, economic and cultural differences of our local surroundings. In 1979, Dubos suggested that ecological consciousness should begin at home. He believed that there needed to be a creation of a World Order in which "natural and social units maintain or recapture their identity, yet interplay with each other through a rich system of communications." In the 1980s, Dubos held to his thoughts on acting locally and felt that issues involving the environment must be dealt with in their "unique physical, climatic and cultural contexts" *(The Encyclopedia of the Environment, Eblen & Eblen, 1994).*

Action at the individual and local level is the first step any of us can take in trying to help improve our communal future. Knut Utstein Kloster believes that the decisions we make, and the actions we take, here and now, right at home, will affect the planet we pass on to future generations. It was for this reason that, throughout his life, he never turned his back on the problems in his community and the challenges right at home, in his backyard. That community heart is a measure of a person's true concern for the larger problems facing society and the planet.

CHAPTER THIRTEEN
Staying Grounded

Knut believes that a world view is not inconsistent with local interests, national pride, and treasuring one's cultural heritage. Many of his activities and accomplishments relate to his Norwegian roots, and to shipping.

Throughout his life, Knut has been an active and contributing member of society in Norway. He was Chairman of the Oslo Shipowners Association and Vice Chairman of the Norwegian Journal of Trade and Shipping. In working with the Norwegian Shipowners Association, Knut chaired several important committees, including one which established a nationwide network of "study groups" and another that was responsible for handling the Association's liaison with society, media policies, educational programs and general industry outreach to foster public understanding of the importance of the shipping industry to the country.

Knut also served as chairman of the Red Cross Building Committee to create an allergy institute in Norway. He pioneered and chaired the planning, design, financing and organization of a residential and service facility for seniors. He sponsored a phonographic record, "Stars on Norway," with Norwegian actress Liv Ullmann, Norwegian broadcaster Erik Bye and many contributing performers in support of a catastrophic fund for world refugees.

He initiated NORSHOW, the Norwegian (Gateway to Scandinavia) pavilion at Epcot Center. He organized and implemented an educational program on shipping for the country's maritime schools and participated in creating the Norwegian Shipping Academy. Knut also initiated and promoted a Norwegian organization for seamen's wives to help them better cope with their husbands' long absences. (In those days, most Norwegian crew were men. Today, many women have taken up the call of the sea.)

Knut represented the shipping industry in LIBERTAS, a national cross-industry organization dedicated to the cause of protecting free enterprise "from creeping socialist encroachment" through a continuous process of providing the public and elected officials information "showing how important free enterprise is in protecting and preserving freedom generally."

He was active in mobilizing community responsibility against juvenile delinquency by creating youth residences, special schools, humanitarian organizations, and clubs to help young people in need. He served on the board of the Norwegian Family Council, dedicated to developing three generational housing projects; he organized hiking programs for school children where they could learn to read maps and use the compass; and he actively supported crisis centers and animal shelters.

Tage Wandborg tells a story about Knut that goes back to

1966 when they were planning for the construction of the *M/S SUNWARD*. A business conference was in session at Klosters Rederi A/S, but Knut was interrupted by his secretary to say that a prisoner was on the telephone, asking to speak with him. Knut had been a regular visitor to the local prison under the auspices of the Red Cross. He had told the prisoners to feel free to call him at any time, day or night, if they needed to speak with him. So when one actually did, he naturally took the call.

Knut also started and chaired the establishment of Industritjeneste A/S — an industrial service enterprise offering jobs to released prisoners who needed a foothold to get back into society.

All of Knut's contributions to shipping and the cruise industry— and his commitments to sustainability, a healthier planet and a better world for all children — accrue in many ways to Norway where his globalist values were born and nurtured.

A few years ago, Knut was awarded the highest honor that can be bestowed on a Norwegian — the Order of St. Olav. Knut received the award for his contribution to the shipping industry in Norway. He felt very uncomfortable about the award, believing that no one person, but rather all of the men and women who have contributed to Norway's shipping industry, should receive such an award. He accepted it only on the basis that it was intended to recognize the contributions of all involved in Norway's important shipping industry.

The Vinland Revisited expedition (Chapter Six) started out as a Norwegian-Icelandic project but expanded when *GAIA* the Viking ship was sent on from Washington to Rio and the Earth Summit. Knut's initial investment involved the acquisition of the replica Viking ship, *GAIA*, and costs associated with her journey

Norwegian school children are joined by British scientist, James Lovelock, his wife Sandy, and Knut Kloster onboard GAIA at Sandefjord.

to Vinland (America). It was Norway's spirit of discovery that motivated the expedition and Knut's participation in the project. He saw how — in today's world — that spirit of discovery could be directed toward discovering better ways to live together in harmony with one another and with Mother Earth. At the end of the *GAIA* to Rio voyage, Knut donated the ship to the municipality of Sandefjord, the location in Norway where the original Gogstad Viking ship was excavated, and she is well cared for there, enjoyed throughout the year by the children and "grown-ups" of the region.

Knut renamed the *S/S FRANCE* the *S/S NORWAY* (Chapter Three), and the ship immediately became part of the country's national heritage. In the summer of 1984, the *S/S NORWAY* visited her adopted homeland. It was an exhilarating cruise up and down Norway's long rugged coastline to the North Cape and the "land of the midnight sun." That was a momentous occasion for Norwegians. Thousands of citizens gathered along her route in the towns and villages she visited, in and out of Norway's many beautiful fjords, and to Oslo, the nation's capital. A virtual flotilla of small- and medium-sized boats accompanied the ship everywhere she went.

In a wonderful book written about the *S/S Norway* and this historic visit,[23] the authors recounted the ship's call at the ancient Hanseatic City of Bergen: "A reigning monarch could not have been given a more enthusiastic welcome," they wrote.

When it was announced that the 1994 Winter Olympics would be held in Norway, Knut was determined to join his fellow countrymen and women to make the event the best it could possibly be. Most importantly, Norwegians wanted to share with the world as much as possible about their country, its history, culture, spirit of discovery, and commitment to nature and the environment.

Norway recognized that the '94 Winter Olympics (OL-94) would be its most significant international event of the decade. Since Norway is often thought of as "an environmental nation" and its Prime Minister at the time, Hon. Gro Harlem Brundtland, was often referred to as "the world's environment minister,"[24] Norway recognized that it had a special responsibility and opportunity to make the '94 Winter Olympics an environmental showcase. Norway has long encouraged international agreements for protection of the environment and for sustainable development, and the organizing committee realized that the eyes of the world would be focused on Norway's own environment and environmental policies, all the more so as

---

[23]*S.S. NORWAY*— A Tribute in Words and Pictures—published by Forlaget Nordvest (1984/85)

[24] Hon. Gro Harlem Brundtland served as chairman of the UN World Commission on Environment and Development which led to the 1992 Earth Summit.

a nation rich in natural resources.

The aim was an "environmentally friendly Olympics" with special attention directed at the construction of environmentally responsible buildings as well as infrastructure development that served the purpose of the Games while preserving the natural environment and having a constructive useful life for Norwegian citizens when the Games were over.

Knut undertook the single largest construction project associated with the Olympics' development — creation of Hafjell village where the global media would be housed during the Olympics at Lillehammer. Again, Knut invoked Gaia, Mother Earth, as the theme of the project. Hafjell was to be a traditional Norwegian village — a twenty-minute drive from the center of Lillehammer and a short walk to the top of the Olympic slalom and downhill ski trails as well as some of Norway's most treasured cross-country skiing and hiking trails. Hafjell was comprised of 225 traditional sod-roofed cottages — in designs dating back centuries — and 125 apartments plus a large community center, Gaiastova, which would be home base to the world's media during the events.

After the Olympics, the cottages and apartments were sold to private individuals and corporations. Today, many Norwegian families come to Hafjell to enjoy the sweeping views of the mountains and the Gudbransdalen Valley below and to enjoy hiking, cross-country and downhill skiing, as well as great memories of the '94 Olympics. Hafjell was one of the most successful development projects associated with the event.

In Chapter Five, *Hands Across the Sea,* Knut's city-ship project was sent abroad for further development and realization in a country which generates over 90% of cruise revenues and which would enable the project to take advantage of additional markets such as coastwise trading and meetings and conferences. Nonetheless, to the extent that the American Flagship project would rely on foreign technology, Knut requested that Norwegian technology be given a preference. "Hands across the sea" was to work both ways, to the extent that Norway — one of the leading maritime nations of the world — could provide products and services that are not available, or as competitively available, in the United States. In this spirit of cooperation, over $100 million worth of Norwegian products and services have been specified for the American Flagship, and Letters of Intent have been entered into to formalize this cooperation. Among the Norwegian companies to benefit from participation in the American Flagship project are Jets Vacuum AS, York-Novenco AS, Autronica Fire and Security AS, Rapp

Bomek AS, Norsk Inova AS, Vincard AS, and NORAC AS.

In May of 1981, Knut was given a plaque by the Sons of Norway for his dedication and service as a member of the Advisory Board. The Sons of Norway was organized by eighteen Norwegian immigrants in Minneapolis, Minnesota in 1895 as a fraternal benefit society. The purposes and goals of the Founding Fathers were to protect members of the Sons of Norway and their families from the financial hardships experienced during times of sickness or death in the family. Over time, the mission of the Sons of Norway was expanded to include the preservation and celebration of Norwegian heritage and culture. It is the largest Norwegian organization outside Norway.

Faithful family fjord horse or brave lion symbol?

The national symbol of Norway for centuries has been a lion. Norway's national shield depicts a golden lion standing upright on his hind legs with a crown on his head, holding up a silver axe. Two lions mark the entrance to the Norwegian Parliament Building in Oslo to symbolically protect the members.

Some Norwegians, including Knut, proposed that a more meaningful and appropriate national symbol for Norway be the Norwegian fjord horse. It is believed that the original fjord horse migrated to Norway and was domesticated over 4,000 years ago. It is a hardy, adaptable and efficient breed; calm and gentle, yet active and gregarious. When asked why the fjord horse would be a more meaningful and appropriate national symbol, Knut said:

> This frugal and persevering small horse has played a
> very important role through hard and difficult times in

bringing the Norwegian people to where we are today. Out on the farms, especially in the rugged western part of the country, the fjord horse was part of the family in a very real sense. The horse is strong enough for heavy work, such as plowing the fields or pulling timber, yet light and fast enough to be a good riding and driving horse. There are many sweet stories about how the family's fjord horse was participating in bringing up the children...teaching them to ride and sit tight, purposely going under a branch that would make the child fall off if he or she wasn't alert and careful; and with the whole family deeply moved at the end, saying goodbye to their beloved friend.

Today, the fjord horse is a favorite at Norwegian riding and therapeutic schools as its generally mild temperament and small size make it suitable for children and disabled individuals.

Not so long ago, Norway was one of the poorest countries in Europe, and life for most people was really tough. We owe a huge debt to the fjord horse and, in many people's view, it should be our national symbol rather than the lion with which we have no real or actual connection.

This fjord horse anecdote tells quite a bit about Knut Utstein Kloster: down-to-earth, practical, seeing and appreciating simple realities, and proposing a national symbol that has some true meaning and significance for the country — the hard-working gentle fjord horse versus the mythical protective lion.

One of Knut's good friends was the late Erik Bye,[25] a prominent Norwegian journalist. Erik Bye wrote a story about Norwegian immigration to America, *Blow, Silver Wind*. With

[25] Erik Bye was a much revered man not only in Norway but also in America where he spent many years. In 2008, a film was released in Norway, GIGANTEN (Giant) about Bye's life and contributions as a journalist, author, poet, producer, broadcaster...and exemplar. A chieftain in Norway's cultural life.

the exception of Ireland, no single country has contributed a larger percentage of her population to America than Norway. Bye's story begins in 1825 with the sailing of the first "immigrant vessel", the sloop *RESTAURATION*, from Stavanger to New York. The story ends with a salute to the *S.S. NORWAY*, also en route to New York, after her triumphant 1984 visit to her adopted homeland. In wishing her 'god seilas' (a happy voyage), Bye writes:

> She represents the strong bonds between our countries
> that have existed ever since the *RESTAURATION* made
> her historic crossing in 1825.

In Bye's story, he suggests that Knud Rasmussen Kloster, our Knut's ancestor, was no doubt present in the crowd that day when the *RESTAURATION* set sail for the New World: "He belonged to an old seafaring family, and it makes sense that his descendants later established their shipping company in that very city."

Hence, the bond between Knut and Norway, Knut and America, and Knut and what he calls "no man's land,"[26] is easy to trace and admire.

This chapter was named "Staying Grounded" because that is an important part of Knut's personal and professional way of life. Although he has undertaken some very challenging enterprises, and some sizable risks, Kloster's feet have never left the ground, except perhaps in elation occasionally, such as when the *S/S NORWAY* was greeted so enthusiastically by the Norwegian people on her maiden voyage there in 1981 (see Chapter Three). Keeping one's feet on the ground is quite an accomplishment for

---

[26] Knut's "no man's land" is defined as "the distance between the world-*that-is* and the world-*as-it should-be*."

a visionary — some would say "dreamer." Knut believes that it is possible to dream and plan great things without surrendering common sense, judgment, and most particularly, values.

You will note that there is very little in this book about politics because, although Knut is very interested in how government works and how it can work better, he sees himself more as a rebel, working outside the system to spur innovation, new thinking, creative problem-solving, and fairness. As an intellectual, he is constantly questioning if the status quo, including, for example, on how and why people vote and what they really think about the governments they have put in place through this political process, is acceptable. Is it the best it can be?

Norway has a multi-party system, making it difficult, if not impossible, for a single party to come into power on its own. Coalitions are generally formed between parties or among several parties. Knut believes that most political parties no longer mirror their political differences so clearly or as deeply as in the past. We see the same thing here in the United States; it's sometimes difficult to distinguish between what the Republicans are advocating and what the Democrats are advocating — often the same thing such as debt reduction, job creation, immigration and healthcare reform. What really differentiates the parties is how they propose to solve these issues. Even here in the U.S., with basically a two-party system, the lines are blurred.

Knut once commissioned a nationwide survey in Norway to find out how people viewed the electoral system. He retained the services of a very reputable Norwegian institution, Markets and Media Institute, to undertake the survey. A simple question was asked. "If there was a general election tomorrow, and, if instead of having only one vote, you had ten votes which you could distribute between the various parties, would you give all your votes to one party, or would you distribute them between several parties?" The result was interesting. About 50% of the respondents said that they would distribute their votes among several parties.

It was interpreted by the Institute that political parties are no longer so clearly associated with a particular or singular political stance, i.e., Conservative, Liberal, Labor, Socialist (right, left, center, etc.), as in the past. The survey also suggested that reforming the system to permit citizens to cast votes for more than one party would have a positive effect on voter participation. "Your votes," Knut said, "could still support a single party, as before, if that's what you wanted. But, as I believed then, and still very much believe, having ten votes for possible distribution would strengthen the democratic election process, making it more meaningful for all concerned, not the least for the political parties themselves."

Obviously, implementation of Knut's good idea would send a much clearer signal to the parties as to what the electorate really wants and expects out of its government, no longer blurred by the politics of coalition. "It wouldn't affect the number of parties," Knut added, "but each party would know which of its attributes and/or positions on issues was being embraced or rejected by a given vote." Clearly such reform would work equally well in the United States. It would be refreshing to know exactly what the citizenry really wanted, issue by issue, rather than having to lump all issues into one hat that is, theoretically, best aligned with one's own choices and political positions.

This is what is meant by "staying grounded" — staying in

contact with reality, staying focused on the issues and processes that matter most, here and now, for everyday citizens.

CHAPTER FOURTEEN
The Future Belongs to Those Who Take It...

In one of his 1976 articles for *KAPITAL*, Knut talked about "Vår fremtid", our future:

> I think it was Aldous Huxley, the British author, who once remarked: "A fact remains a fact even if you choose to ignore it." The fact we are facing today, which increasingly will set the stage for developing countries in years to come, is that they will no longer accept the rules of the game set by the "elite class of nations." These rules have stamped the economic and trade political development over the last 500 years ever since Vasco da Gama gave Europe a footing in Africa and India and up until the fall of 1973 when the counter wave came from the OPEC countries. The rules of the game are now in the melting pot; they will surely be radically changed as time moves on.***
>
> The sooner we get started with the process of leveling the field between rich and poor countries, the better it will be for the development of a healthy world trade.*** I think we ought to engage ourselves actively, industry-wise, in the process of setting the stage for the development of

> a new economic global system — a system which will
> challenge our traditional thinking by giving the great
> majority of the world's people a concrete experience, at
> long last, of getting a "fair deal."

It was Adlai Stevenson, back in 1953, who said that the future belongs to those who take it. A half century later, we know that if we do not take hold of the future, it will take hold of us.

Knut has always clearly seen that a "fair deal" for every man, woman and child on the planet is the only path to peace and prosperity. He has seen that Mother Nature demands nothing less than that from her inhabitants — a fair deal: that we share her bounty, respect her rules, preserve her natural resources, protect the delicate balance between air, water, land and life, and give back more than we take from her during our time on Earth.

Each of us, of course, must follow our own light, our own star, our own inner compass. But we share a common future — or a common fate. Knut's story shows how we can use our time, talents, experience, business ventures and knowledge — our hearts and our heads — to take hold of the future and steer a healthier, more equitable, and sustainable course forward. When asked about the "flickering soul" metaphor, used in his 1981 speech at the Norwegian-American Chamber of Commerce (Chapter Eight), which is used in the subtitle of this book, Knut wrote:

> In Norwegian, it is "flakkende sjel." I just looked
> up "flakkende" in the dictionary, and there it was,
> "flickering." "Sjel" and "soul" was easy. So there it is,
> flickering soul. And it *does* hurt. I wonder if it isn't how
> billions of people around the world feel, when you
> get right down to what it means to be a human being.

> Whether you are so-called rich or poor. No man's land is
> where you are, in your heart and mind, and/or between
> right and left, and/or in believing or not believing in
> the divine creation, wanting to do the right thing — but
> overwhelmed by the enormity of the challenge.

We can't "stop the world" because we want to "get off" — to borrow from the popular 1966 Broadway musical. But we can make a difference. We can help create a better future. It is not a matter of being a big financial success, making a big splash, or how often one is seen in the media. But rather, using the opportunities we have and the work we are doing to help bridge that huge gap between the world-*as-it-is* and the world-*as-it-should-be*. That is what Knut Utstein Kloster has done his entire life. We possess the scientific and technological resources to solve the world's problems and to construct a positive future for all its citizens. The challenge of our time is to find ways to apply these resources to basic human needs on a global scale and to integrate scientific and technological advances with human values and global ethics. Millions of individuals and organizations and institutions around the world are devoted to this task.

Knut Utstein Kloster is just one flickering soul, one candle in the dark, one star in the firmament. His projects — those which have been realized and those that will be realized in the future — are all examples of how every step we take can merge practical and idealistic objectives. We can all make a difference simply by caring and following our own True North.

CHAPTER FIFTEEN

Space to Grow

In 1966, Knut sent *M/S SUNWARD* to Miami and launched Norwegian Caribbean Lines (NCL). Soon there were four ships and the cruise industry was born (see Chapter One).

"When *SUNWARD* came to Miami," Knut recently wrote, "she did indeed create the space for growth all around her. Great opportunities for business development and job creation, locally and in the Caribbean. Travel trade, port development, ship operations and associated businesses."

With Naval Architect Tage Wandborg, Knut broke the mold fifteen years after introducing *M/S SUNWARD* with the conversion of the *S/S FRANCE* to the *S/S NORWAY* (Chapter Three), taking passenger count from 500-800 to 2,400 guests. Now, four decades after it all began, Kloster and Wandborg are introducing the optimum cruise ship, *AMERICA WORLD CITY* at 265,000 GRT.

"We've seen the cruise industry grow from NCL's four ship 'White Fleet,'" Kloster observes, "to over 200 cruise ships operating today under various brands; and the size of ships has grown from *SUNWARD's* 8,666 GRT to NCL's *EPIC* at 155,873 GRT and RCI's *OASIS* and *ALLURE* at 225,000 GRT."

"Space to grow, this is what the American Flagship project is all about," Knut says. "Space to grow — space to create thousands of new jobs, billions in new tax revenues, and exciting new economic activity along America's beautiful coastline, from Portland to Galveston and New Orleans; from Seattle to San Diego."

In their marketing materials, America World City Inc. calls America's territorial waters "The Fifty-First State — a virgin market reserved under U.S. law for American-flag floating resorts." The Fifty-First State includes 25 metropolitan areas, 12 of America's top tourist destinations, and a population of over 100 million people within an hour's drive of a place where they can embark or disembark from *AMERICA WORLD CITY.*

"It will happen all over again," Knut confidently predicts, "just what happened many years ago when *M/S SUNWARD* came to Miami and pioneered the creation of space for the cruise industry to grow."

"The introduction of an American-flag ship, the world's largest passenger ship, will take the cruise industry into the future and grow the American economy through job creation, port and coastal development, construction, and myriad service and supply industries," Knut says.

When we discussed this Second Edition of the book, Knut sent me a photo of the original brass bell from *SUNWARD's* bridge. It hangs outside his little office hut at Hvaler, a summer cottage. He said it reminds him of the past as well as the future, and it highlights for him the "space to grow" concept.

"It's more than a business pursuit," he said:

> It is two very meaningful words put together. A truly
> bipartisan concept, in a global perspective. As human
> beings, with all kinds of backgrounds, interests and
> activities, we all need space to grow, whoever we are,
> wherever we live, whatever we do, and whatever we
> believe in. That's human nature. Rich and poor, man and
> woman, young and old. All on the same existential high
> road. I look at the bell from *SUNWARD* and I think of
> John Donne's poem, 'For Whom the Bell Tolls' — that we
> are all in this together, our past and our future.

I like Knut's "space to grow" idea. It can be applied to our
personal lives as much as to our professional aspirations. It's
fascinating to think that little *M/S SUNWARD* started what is
today a $40 billion industry. But it is even more fascinating to
think that, in terms of the American economy and job creation,
we have yet to begin. While 90%+ of cruise passengers are

Americans generating $40 billion in revenues — sailing out of mostly U.S. ports on foreign-built, foreign-flagged, foreign-crewed ships — there is not one major U.S.-built, U.S.-flagged, U.S.-crewed ocean-going cruise ship. Not one.

All that is about to change.

AMERICA WORLD CITY is, to the U.S. economy, what *SUNWARD* was to the cruise industry: the beginning of an exciting, lucrative, job-creating new industry. Space to grow right here at home, harnessing our own markets, capitalizing on our own passengers, building our own ships, sailing "floating cities" domestically along our own coastline, and putting our own officers, crew and hospitality workers BACK to WORK.

Thank you, True North. We finally get it.

EPILOGUE

"In life we find many men that are great, and some that are
good, but very few men are both great and good."
— Charles Caleb Colton

I was motivated to write this book because I had the pleasure
and privilege of knowing such a man.

In 2007, the Cruise Line International Association (CLIA),
North America's cruise industry organization, honored Knut by
inducting him into the Hall of Fame as a pioneer of the cruise
industry. In accepting the award for him, I spoke of Knut's less
known pioneering in another field — the field of "doing well by
doing good." I talked about his vision for the cruise industry and
how it might play an important role in helping to shape a better
future, particularly in terms of protecting the environment. I said
that Knut hopes the ships of the future will become high profile
examples of new energy-efficient technologies and as learning
platforms where its passengers can enjoy their vacations along
with increased awareness of, and participation in, programs and

projects aimed at improving themselves and the world around them. The approximately 2,000 delegates attending CLIA's Hall of Fame event, consisting mostly of travel agents (the backbone of the cruise industry), seemed to embrace the message. It was a good night, and I was extremely proud of Knut for his impact on the industry — past, present, and future.

Left to right: Andrew Stuart, Executive Vice President, Global Sales and Passenger Services for Norwegian Cruise Line; Stephanie Gallagher; Brad Anderson, Co-President of America's Vacation Center; Terry Dale, President of CLIA at the time.

PHOTO CREDITS

INDEX